THE
HISTORY OF JAHANGIR

THE HISTORY OF JAHANGIR

FRANCIS GLADWIN

GYAN

Published by

Gyan Publishing House
5, Ansari Road
Daryaganj, New Delhi-110002
Phone: 011-47034999, 9811692060
E-mail: books@gyanbooks.com

Distribution Network
gyanbooks.com
India, USA, Canada, UK, Australia

ISBN: 978-93-7014-069-1 (PB)

First Published, 1930

2nd Impression 2025

Printed at: Gyan Press, Delhi.

THE HISTORY OF JAHANGIR
Author: FRANCIS GLADWIN

JAHANGIR

THE HISTORY OF JAHANGIR

By FRANCIS GLADWIN

EDITED WITH NOTES BY

Rao Bahadur

K. V. RANGASWAMI AIYANGAR, M. A.

PRINCIPAL, H. H. THE MAHARAJA'S COLLEGE OF ARTS, TRIVANDRUM

PUBLISHERS:

B. G. PAUL & CO. MADRAS

CONTENTS

INTRODUCTION

THE history of the reign of Jahangir now reprinted was published in 1788. Its author Francis Gladwin had a considerable reputation in his day as an accomplished Persian scholar and translator. Between 1783 and 1786 he published a valuable translation of Abul Fazl's famous Ain-i-Akbari. The success of the translation encouraged him to persevere in his researches in the history of the successors of Akbar. He planned a large work which was "to attempt a delineation of the most material changes that happened in the constitution of Hindostan during the reign of Jehangir, Shahjehan and Aurungazebe". He apparently wrote out the bulk, if not the whole, of this work, to judge from the reference to the later parts of it in the perface to the first volume of the large history, which alone was published.

Gladwin's History is thus a fragment, but it is complete as far as the reign of Jahangir is concerned. His translation of the Ain-i-Akbari was brought out under the patronage of Warren Hastings who warmly commended it to the Board of Directors. This famous translation is still useful, and is, in fact, owing to the availability of a cheap reprint published some years ago in Calcutta, now the only easily accessible English translation, the magistral annotated translation begun by H. Blochmann and completed by Colonel H. S. Jarrett, which superseded Gladwin's translation, having long been out of print. That Gladwin's translation of the Ain-i-Akbari is still of value is evidenced by the publication a few years ago of a supplement to it prepared by Dr. Rushbrook Williams for the use of students studying the political and economic organization of the Mughal Empire.

Like Anderson, Halhed and Hamilton, Gladwin benefited largely from the discerning patronage of Warren Hastings. It is probable that the departure of Warren Hastings from India is the main cause of the failure of Gladwin to complete the projected History of Akbar's successors. The 'History of Jehangir' is dedicated to Lord Cornwallis. Its success in a commercial sense does not appear to have been great. The slim quarto volume passed out of print very soon, and it has since remained one of the scarcer 18th century contributions to Indian History in the oriental book-market of to-day. Its title seldom appears in the price-lists issued by the leading second-hand booksellers. Its value as a sober and accurate account of the reign of Jahangir was recognised by the late Dr. Vincent Smith, but hitherto students of Indian history have been unable to obtain it owing to the prohibitive prices commanded by copies occasionally offered for sale. It is with a view to make this rare and useful work accessible to students of Indian history that the publishers have now arranged to issue this reprint.

Very little is known of the personal history of Gladwin. In the preface to the work now reprinted he refers to his 23 years' residence in India. As the preface is dated August 1788, Gladwin would appear to have come out to India about 1765. It is known that he began his career in the service of the East India Company as an officer of the Bengal Army. He showed from the commencement of his service a passion for oriental studies and a remarkable aptitude for the mastery of languages. He pursued the study of oriental literatures with steadfastness and zeal. His reputation as an orientalist, and particularly as a Persian scholar was soon well established. Under the inspiration of Warren Hastings, whose newly-founded Asiatic Society, Gladwin joined on its foundation in 1783, the famous translation of the Ain-i-Akbari was prepared and published in three substantial volumes between 1783 and 1786. Subsequent to the publication of his fragmentary history of Akbar's successors in 1788, Gladwin published "An Account of the transactions in Bengal during the Viceroyships of Assim-Us-Shan and Alavardikhan," some translations of the major Persian Classics like the Gulistan, a Persian Hindusthani Dictionary and a number of vocabularies and works on grammar dealing with Indian languages.

In 1801 the Marquis of Wellesly appointed Gladwin as the first Professor of Persian in the famous College of Fort William which was founded for the purpose of enabling the members of the

East India Company's Civil Service to obtain suitable instruction in the languages, literatures and the history of India. Gladwin took his duties as a professor very seriously, and made a great and well merited reputation as an instructor of infective enthusiasm. He also made many plans for further literary work. Among these was one for the publication of carefully edited and annotated Persian Classics. For this purpose he even prepared new founts of oriental types which he presented to the College. After 1802 Gladwin appears to have obtained a more lucrative place in the Company's Service as Collector of Customs and subsequently Commissary Resident at Patna. No publication of his can be traced after 1809. Very little is known of his declining years. He is presumed to have died on or about the year 1813 when a probate of his will was issued.

Gladwin's History merits republication not only on account of its scarcity but also on account of its excellence as a sober, scholarly work based on a careful study of the original sources in Persian. Gladwin refers in the Preface to his History, with pardonable pride, to the value of his collections of Persian historical manuscripts "purchased at great expense" during a period of nearly quarter of a century. Gladwin's acuteness is shown by the excellent use which he has made of the manuscripts of the authentic biography of Jahangir, at a time when the spurious version of it was acclaimed to be the original of the famous autobiography. James Anderson had indeed brought the authentic version to the notice of scholars by publishing translations of some extracts from it in 1786. But, till the publication of the monumental 'History of India as told by its historians', by Sir Henry Elliot and Professor John Dowson, the value of the authentic Memoirs was not properly appreciated. In 1864 an edition of the Memoirs was published by Syed Ahmed Khan under the title of 'Tuzuk-i-Jahangir'. The first volume of a scholarly English translation of the Memoirs was published by Mr. H. Beveridge in 1909. The translation was completed in 1914 by the publication of the second volume by Colonel Rogers.

The spurious Memoirs appeared about three years after Jahangir's death. It was this work which was translated by Major David Price of the Bombay Army. Price's translation appeared in 1829 as a volume published under the Oriental Translation Fund. For many years an animated controversy raged over the question of the authenticity of the rival versions of the Memoirs, and leading Persian scholars like De Sacy, Rieu, Morley, Elliot and Dowson took part in the discussion. The controversy is now at an end. Scholars are agreed now that the version which Price translated does not represent the authentic autobiography Its confused arrangement, errors of statement, extravagant language, digressions, and paucity of dates show that as a literary and historical work it is decidedly inferior to the authentic version. The uncomplimentary references to Shahjahan found in the authentic version are absent in the spurious. This is obviously due to the circumstance that the mangled version appeared during the reign of Shahjahan. The genuine Memoirs were published in his lifetime, with the approval of Jahangir. They are now known to exist in two issues. The first of these, as recorded in the work itself, carries the narrative only to the end of the 12th year of the reign. It is to these Memoirs that Gladwin refers in the following passage:

> "They contain a minute account of the political and private conduct of his (Jehangir's) life from the commencement of his reign to the end of the twelfth year. They are universally admired for the purity, elegance and simplicity of the style and he appears in general to have exposed his own follies and weaknesses with great candour and fidelity. When he had completed the Memoirs of twelve years, he distributed several copies of them amongst his children and the principal officers of his Court. He continued these Memoirs with his own hand till the commencement of the seventeenth year of his reign, when finding himself, from ill-health, unable to proceed, he from that period to the time of his death, employed Mutamed Khan as his amanuensis. The whole of the continuation is exceedingly scarce; the compiler of this history not having been able to procure the sight of any other copy than the one which was lent to him by his friend Colonel Polier."

With reference to the above passage, it may be noted that Mutamad Khan was commissioned by the Emperor, whose health was then breaking down, to prepare the Memoirs only from the seventeenth to the nineteenth year. This is the second issue of the genuine Memoirs. It brings the narrative from the accession to the nineteenth year of the reign.

The merit of Gladwin's History consists in his careful study of virtually all the sources available to the student of the history of the reign of Jahangir. Though annalistic in form and written in an unornate and pedestrian style, the History is redeemed from dulness by the good sense and critical acumen of the author. Gladwin claimed that the reader might rely on the fidelity of the compilation. The close examination of the History and a comparison of it with the extant sources will show that this claim is justified. A perusal of the footnotes added to the present reprint will show how in very few instances alone Gladwin's statements require modification in the light of later research. Gladwin's style does not lack clearness or force. His narrative runs on without effort and maintains the equable dignity and brevity of the originals which it follows. The limitations imposed on himself in regard to the treatment of the subject have unfortunately stood in the way of Gladwin's attempting a critical discussion of some of the more intriguing problems of Jahangir's reign, such as the treatment of Khusru, the murder of Sher Afghan, the character of Nur Jahan, etc. The discussions of these topics would have enhanced the value of the History. But Gladwin has tried to make up for such omissions by giving a short but essentially just estimate of Jahangir's character and attainments. On several questions he has provided us only with his verdicts without revealing the grounds on which they were based. Judged in the light of recent research Gladwin's conclusions will be found to be singularly valid and to vindicate the quality of his critical power. Probably the only point on which a modern student would quarrel with Gladwin is his unfavourable characterisation of Nur Jahan and his readiness to attribute her public acts to ignoble motives.

At a time when interest in the critical study of Indian History has become general, it is unnecessary to justify the publication of the reprint of a work of this character. In order that this reprint might be more useful to students, notes have been added giving references to original and secondary sources of information. A list of the principal authorities has also been given. The original punctuation and spelling of proper names and Persian words have naturally been retained. In the preparation of the edition and particularly of the notes, which have entailed considerably more trouble and more labour than their number and length would indicate, I have been greatly assisted by Mr. T. M. Krishnamachari, M.A., B.L., Professor of History, H. H. The Maharajha's College of Arts, Trivandrum, and by my son and pupil Mr. K. R. Padmanabha Aiyangar, M.A., B.L., of the Indian Audit and Accounts Service.

TRIVANDRUM,
12th September 1930.

K. V. RANGASWAMI

LIST OF ABBREVIATIONS USED IN THE FOOTNOTES TO THE TEXT

A. N. ... *Akbarnama* by Abul Fazl translated by H. Beveridge.

E. D. ... Sir Henry Elliot and Professor John Dowson's *History of India as told by its own Historians* 1867-77.

Iqbal ... *Iqbalnama-i-Jahangiri* by Motamad Khan (Bibliotheca Indica) 1865.

J. B. A. S. ... Journal of the Asiatic Society of Bengal.

J. R. A. S. ... Journal of the Royal Asiatic Society.

Khaf ... Khafikhan's *Muntakhab-ul-lubab* (Bibliotheca Indica), 1869.

Maasir ... *Maasir-ul-Umara* by Shah Nawaz Khan published by the Bengal Asiatic Society in three parts and being translated into English.

M. J. ... *Maasiri Jahangiri* by Khwaja Kamgar Husain.

Firish ... *Tarikhi-Hind* by Muhammad Qasim Hindu Shah translated by Briggs in 4 vols. in 1829.

R. B. ... *Tuzuk-i-Jahangiri* translated into English in two volumes by Rogers and revised and edited by Beveridge, 1909—1914.

Price ... Memoirs of Jahangir (spurious memoirs) translated by Major D. Price.

Takmil ... *Takmil-i-Akbarnama* by Inayat-ullah.

CHIEF AUTHORITIES CITED IN THE NOTES

Akbarnama—by Abul Fazl published since 1897 and translated by Henry Beveridge.

Ain-i-Akbari—by Abul Fazl translated by H. Blochman and Col. Jarraett in 3 vols. Calcutta 1878, 1891, 1894.

Takmil-i-Akbarnama—by Inayat Ullah continuing Abul Fazl's work from 1602 to 1605.

Muntakhab-ut-Tawarikh—by Abdul Qadir Badauni translated into English in three parts by Col. Ranking; W. H. Lowo (revised by E. B. Cowell); and Col. Haig respectively (Bibliotheca Indica) the last being yet incomplete.

The Wiqaya—by Asad Beg, servant of Abul Fazl.

Anfaul Akhbar—by Muhammad Amin.

Tarikhi Firishta—by Muhammad Qasim Hindu Shah (Firishta) translated by Briggs in 4 vols. in 1829.

Tuzuk-i-Jahangiri—Memoirs of Jahangir (genuine) published by Sayyid Ahmad Khan, 1864 translated by A Rogers and revised and edited by Henry Beveridge in 2 vols. London 1909—1914.

Tarikh-i-Salim Shahi—Memoirs of Jahangir translated by Major David Price (1829) [reprinted by the Bangabasi Press Calcutta, 1906,]—This is a famous translation of the spurious version.

Iqbalnama Jahangiri—by Motamad Khan, Text (Bibliotheca Indica), 1865.

Maasir-i-Jahangiri—by Khwaja Kamgar Husain (Khuda Baksh M. S.).

Khulasat-ut-Tawarikh—by Sujan Rai.

Muntakhab-ul-lubab—by Muhammad Hashim Khafi Khan (Bibliotheca Indica), 1869.

Tatimma Waqiat Jahangiri—by Muhammad Hadi in Elliot and Dowson, Vol. VI.

Maasir-ul-umara—by Shah Nawaz Khan published by the Bengal Asiatic Society.

History of India as told by its own Historians—by Sir H. M. Elliot and J. Dowson, in 8 vols., London, 1867—77.

Mongolicae legation is commentarius—of Father Anthony Monserrate, edited by Father Hosten and translated into English by J. S. Hoyland, Oxford University Press, 1922.

Akbar and the Jesuits—Part of his larger work '*Thesaurus etc.*' by Father Pierre Du Jarrie, translated with notes by C. H. Payney, Routledge, 1926.

Jesuit Missions to Emperor Akbar—by E. D. Maclagan, in J. A. S. B. Part I, Vol. LXV, 1896, pp. 38-113.

Jahangir's India—by Francisco Pelsart, translated by W. H. Moreland and Dr. Geyl-Heffer, 1925.

Embassy of Sir Thomas Roe to India—Edited by William Foster, new edition, revised and illustrated, Oxford University Press, 1926.

Voyage to East India—by the Rev. Edward Terry, London, 1777.

Travels of Pietro Della Valle—translated and edited by Edward Grey, 2 Vols. Hakluyt Society, 1891.

'*De Imperio Magni Mogali's...*'—by John De Laet. First part translated by Lethbridge in the Calcutta Review, 1870 and 1871.

Letters received by the East India Company from its servants in the East—6 vols. 1602—1617. Edited by Danvers and Foster, London, 1896—1902.

'Observations of William Finch, merchant, taken out of his large journal' in Purchas IV, pp 1-77.

The English Factories in India—1618—1629. Edited by William Foster. London, 1906—09.

Travels of Peter Mundy Vol. II—Edited by R. C. Temple. Hakluyt Society 1907—1914.

Travels in India—by Jean Baptiste Tavernier edited by V. Ball in 2 volumes 1889.

Travels in the Mughal Empire, 1656—58—by M. Francois Bernier translated by A. Constable, London, 1914.

Storio do Mogor, 1653—1708, by Niccolo Manucci translated by Irvine in 4 Vols.

'*The Annals and Antiquities of Rajasthan*'—by James Todd 2 Vols. Routledge.

Moghul Architecture of Fathpur Sikri—described and illustrated by E. W. Smith, Government Press, Allahabad, 1894—1898.

Old Title

THE HISTORY OF HINDOSTAN

DURING THE REIGNS OF

JEHANGIR, SHAHJEHAN,

AND

AURUNGZEBE

BY

FRANCIS GLADWIN, Esq.

VOLUME THE FIRST

TO THE RIGHT HONOURABLE

CHARLES EARL CORNWALLIS,

KNIGHT OF THE MOST NOBLE ORDER OF THE GARTER,

GOVERNOR-GENERAL OF INDIA,

&c. &c. &c.

THIS WORK

IS RESPECTFULLY DEDICATED,

BY HIS LORDSHIP'S

MOST OBEDIENT,

AND

MOST HUMBLE SERVANT,

THE AUTHOR

CALCUTTA,

15th of Aug. 1788.

ERRATA

Page 38, foot-note 2, l. 1. *for* " Khurm's " *read* " Khurram's "

" 44, foot-note 4, l. 1. *after* Khusru *insert* a comma

" 45, line 25. *for* " shwon " *read* " shown "

" 47, " 27. *for* " perhunnah " *read* " pergunnah "

" 61, foot-note 2, l. 1. *for* " brough " *read* " brought "

" 70, line 14. *for* " enraged " *read* " engaged "

" 75, " 12. *for* " been " *read* " seen "

" 87, " 28. *before* " along " *add* " stopped "
for " Elemaded dowlah " *read* " Etemaded-dowlah "

" 90, l. 8. *for* " began " *read* " begun "

" 102, l. 25. *for* " be at " *read* " bear "

" 138, l. 7. *for* " Meet " *read* " Meer "

" 142, l. 18. *for* " Mafir " *read* " Masir "

" 148, l. 12. *for* " sirmaun " *read* " firmaun "

" 152, l. 12. *for* " days " *read* " years "

" 158, l, 25. *for* " Khelaffut " *read* " Khelassut "

PREFACE

THE Moghul Empire, in Hindostan, did not obtain any regular form till the reign of Akber. Timour was only an invader. Baber possessed little more than Lahoor and Cabul. Hemayun was expelled by Shere Khan; and lived but a few months after having recovered his kingdom, by the defeat of Secunder Sour, the son and successor of that usurper. Akber, at the age of thirteen, succeeded to the peaceful inheritance of his father's dominions; and, during his minority, the Government acquired vigour, new provinces were conquered, commerce flourished, the finances were improved and disbursements regulated, through the activity and valour, the wisdom, integrity and economy of Byram Khan, the Ameer ul Omrah. When the Emperor assumed the management of affairs, he pursued the wise plans of Byram Khan; and after the experience of thirty-seven years, with the assistance of an upright and most able minister, reduced his observations to a regular system. His Institutes, drawn up by the great Abulfazel, are a lasting monument of their united fame. The skill and sagacity displayed in these arrangements, for every department, with the regard shewn throughout for the security of the life and property of the meanest peasant, give us an high idea of the Government; and it astonishes us to hear the minister of an absolute prince, bred up in a faith notorious for its intolerant spirit, discussing with freedom the rights of humanity; boldly reprobating persecution, and maintaining that the Almighty is the common parent of all mankind. But we contemplate with still higher admiration and reverence, the monarch, who in opposition to the prevailing maxims of despotism, could not only adopt such enlarged sentiments himself, but have the generosity to authorise their promulgation, in order to diffuse general happiness by establishing peace and unanimity amongst his subjects of such opposite persuasions, as the followers of the Bedes, and those of the Mohammedan faith. The one, mild and forgiving, refusing proselytes, but professing an universal philanthropy; the other fierce and vindictive, making converts with the sword; despising and persecuting all those who embrace not their particular creed; pursuing with unrelenting fury, even those amongst themselves, who differ but in the most immaterial point, regarding them as absolute infidels, the objects of their scorn and utter detestation.

The candour and indulgence which I have experienced, in the publication of my translation of the Ayeen Akbery, both here and in Europe, embolden me to attempt a delineation of the most material changes that happened in the constitution of Hindostan, during the succeeding reigns of Jehangir, Shahjehan and Aurungzebe.

The materials for this work are taken from authentic Persian manuscripts, of which I have an ample collection, purchased at a very great expense, during twenty-three years residence in India. The English reader may rely upon the fidelity of this compilation; and for the satisfaction of the Orientalist, whenever I have met with any edict, law or regulation, particularly important, curious and interesting, I have given the original along with the translation, in an appendix, at the end of each reign. Those of Jehangir and Shahjehan afford only few instances of innovation or reform; but the reign of Aurungzebe furnishes many important documents; as, under the Government of that monarch, the constitution of Hindostan was publicly declared (what was before only implied) to be founded on the strictest principles of Mohammedanism; and in these edicts the landed property and other rights of the subject are clearly stated; many points relative to the prerogative of the crown are accurately defined; and the officers of Government fully instructed in the nature and extent of their respective duties.

From the consideration that under Aurungzebe the empire attained to its fullest vigour, I have deferred, till the conclusion of his reign, my remarks on the progressive state of Hindostan, and particularly of the revenues, from the accession of Jehangir; and by observing this method, I am enabled to place the whole in a clear and comprehensive point of view.

Impressed with the warmest sense of gratitude to my honourable employers, to my particular friends, and to the public in general, for their liberal encouragement of my former labours, I pursue my present task with ardour, alacrity and satisfaction; and shall be happy if my endeavours herein may entitle me to the continuance of their favour, approbation and support.

FRANCIS GLADWIN

PARTICULAR EVENTS.

DURING THE REIGN OF AKBER RELATING TO

SULTAN SILEEM.

When the Emperor Akber entered the twenty-ninth year of his age, being very unhappy at not having a son, he went to the village of Sikry, about ten cose distance from Agra, to pay a visit to Sheikh Sileem, a celebrated derveish, and in his presence made a vow, that if Heaven granted him that blessing, he would perform a pilgrimage, on foot, from Agra to the shrine of Khojeh Moyeneddeen Cheisty in the city of Ajmeer. The derveish assured him, that Heaven had listened to his prayers, and would bestow upon him three sons. Akber rejoiced exceedingly at these tidings, and promised that his first-born should be committed to the care of Sheikh Sileem and, accordingly, when one of his Begums[1] was far advanced in her pregnancy, he sent her to the house of the Sheikh, at Sikry, where on Wednesday the 17th of Reby ul Awwel, A. H. 977, or 29th of August 1569, she was delivered of a prince, whom Akber named Sultan Sileem, and who was afterwards the Emperor Jehangir.[2] On this happy occasion, public rejoicings were made throughout the Empire; Akber bestowed magnificent presents upon his courtiers;

[1] For her name see Sujan Rai (1918), p. 374; Beveridge (J.A.S.B. 1887 I 164-7).

[2] Price (Bangabasi edition 1904) adopts A.H. 978; Abul Fazl (Beveridge II 503) gives 30th August and the Tuzuk (R.B. I 2) 31st August. See Badauni (Lowe) II, 124; Nizamud-din Ahmad (E.D.V., 334).

distributed considerable sums in charity, and ordered all prisoners to be set at liberty.[1]*

About five months after the birth of the prince, Akber prepared for fulfilling his vow, by making a pilgrimage on foot, from Agra to the shrine of Moyeneddeen Cheisty, one hundred and forty cose, which he divided into twelve stages.[2] He set out on the 12th of Shaban, or 19th of January 1570, and at the end of seventeen days arrived at the shrine, where he offered up his prayer and thanksgiving with fervent devotion. This renowned Mohammedan saint[3] was born in Seistan, from whence he is sometimes styled Sanjary. His father, Khojeh Hassan, dying at the time he was only fifteen years old, he sought the protection of Sheikh Ibrahim Kundoozy. When he arrived at manhood, he travelled to Samarcand and Bokhara, and from thence to Khorasan, where, in the town of Haroon dependant upon Nishapoor, he became a pupil of Sheikh Osman Haroony, with whom he lived, under a very austere discipline, for twenty years; and then, by the advice of his teacher, he travelled into far countries, and visited the most famous doctors and holy men of that age. Sheikh Moyeneddeen was the grandson of Sheikh Mowdood Cheisty and in him that family became extinct.

From Ajmeer the Emperor went to Delhi, where he arrived in the month of Ramzan, and paid his devotions at the tomb of Hemayun and

[1] Akbarnama (Beveridge) II, 504-5.
* Masir Jehangiry.
[2] Akbarnama (Beveridge) II, 502-3; 510-11; R.B.I. 1, 2, Badauni (Lowe) II, 127; Firishtah (Briggs) II, 33; Nizamuddin (E.D.) V. 334.
[3] Badauni (Haig) III, 87.

other holy shrines in that neighbourhood. From thence he proceeded to Agra, and got back to that city on the 6th of Zilkadeh, or the 11th of April, 1570.

Two years afterwards, upon the conquest of Gujerat, the Emperor in commemoration of that event, as well as for the good fortune which had befallen him at Sikry, founded there a city, to which he gave the name of Futtehabad;[1] and many of the nobility erecting magnificent houses on that spot, in the course of fourteen or fifteen years, it became very populous.*

As soon as the prince was four years, four months and four days old,[2] Mollana Meerkillan Heravee was appointed his tutor, and Katib Mohammed his etaleek, or governor; and when the latter was sent upon a military expedition, that office was conferred upon Mirza Khan-khanan.[3] Four years after this, the Emperor appointed the prince a munsebdar of ten thousand effective cavalry.* When he arrived at his fifteenth year,[4] he was married to the daughter[5] of Bhogwandoss, one of the most powerful Rajahs of Hindustan. The next year he married

[1] On the architecture of Fathpur Sikri E. W. Smith has produced five profusely illustrated volumes in the Archaeological Survey of India. See also R. B. I, 2; Monserrate, pp. 30-2; A. N. II, 503; Badauni III (Haig), 18-27.

* Toozek Jehangiry, or Jehangir's Commentaries, written by himself.

[2] A.N. III, 105-6; Badauni (Lowe) II, 173; Nizamuddin (E.D.V. 370.)

[3] Abdur Rahim Khan, son of Bairam Khan.

* For a particular account of munsebs, or military dignities, *vide* Ayeen Akbery, Vol. I, page 142.

[4] More exactly when he was 15 years, 5 months and 13 days old.

[5] Man Bai. Raja Mansingh was the adopted son of Bhagwandoss, and the uncle of Man Bai's son Prince Khusru.

the daughter of Rajah Oudy Singh,[1] son of the great Row Maldeo, whose army consisted of eighty thousand men, and who gained several victories over the Ranna of Chittore. Within a year after his marriage with the daughter of Bhogwandoss, she was delivered of a princess, who was called Sultana ul Nissa Begum ;[2] and the following year she was brought to bed of a son to whom Akber gave the name of Sultan Khusru.[3] About this time Sultan Sileem took for his third wife, the daughter of Khojeh Hassan, who brought him Sultan Purveiz.[4] He now married a fourth wife, the daughter of Keysoodoss by whom he had a princess named Bahar Bana Begum. Two months subsequent Sultan Khorum,[5] afterwards Shahjehan, was born at Lahoor, of the daughter of Rajah Oudy Singh.*

When Akber marched to the Dekhan, he sent Sultan Sileem into Ajmeer with a powerful army, to make war upon the Ranna of Chittore. Raja Mansingh, Shah Kuly Khan, and others of the principal nobility were left with the prince. Rajah Mansingh, although at this time Soobahdar of Bengal, was prevailed upon to go against the Ranna; and appointed his brother, Juggetsingh, for the management of his government; but he dying shortly after, his son, Mahasingh, succeeded him in that trust. The prince sent forward Rajah

[1] A. N. II, 677-8 ; Badauni (Lowe) II, 352.
[2] R. B. I, 15 ; Price 35 ; Khaf. I, 245.
[3] R. B. I, 18-9 ; Price 33.
[4] R. B. I, 18-9. Two years and two months after Khusru.
[5] R.B. I, 18-9.
* Masir Jehangiry.

Mansingh with the army, and followed himself by slow marches, hunting all the way, till he arrived at Oudypoor. The Ranna after some skirmishes with the imperial troops, fled to the mountains, and no advantage was gained over him, but taking some prisoners.[1]

At this juncture Mansingh received such intelligence from Bengal as made him desirous to return thither, in order to quell the disturbances occasioned by his absence; and thinking the present state of affairs favourable for his brother-in-law, Sileem, he advised him to take advantage of the Emperor's being engaged in foreign conquests, which might detain him a long time, and possess himself of all the provinces on the east of the river, Ganges.[2] Sileem, seduced by the evil counsel of Mansingh, and supported by the advice of some other courtiers, gave up the pursuit of the Ranna, and marched back to Agra.[3] Kheleej Khan, the killadar of Agra, unsuspecting of danger, came out to pay his respects to the prince, whose partisans advised him to detain that officer, till he consented to deliver up the fort, which contained all the imperial treasure;[4] an acquisition that could not fail of raising the possessor to the throne. But he rejected this advice, and after receiving the compliments of Kheleej Khan, gave him leave to return to Agra; and then proceeded with his army to Allahabad. Miriam Mekany, the Emperor's mother, being

[1] A. N. III, 831; Khaf. 1, 216.

[2] A. N. Text III, 831; E.D. VI, 98-9; Maasiri Jahangiri, p. 15.

[3] M. J. p., 13.

[4] which amounted to 20 million at Akbar's death according to the Jesuits.

informed of Sileem's intentions, went out to meet him to endeavour to dissuade him from so rash an enterprise. But Sileem, in order to avoid her, set off for Allahabad in a light boat; and the Begum, disappointed in her purpose, returned to Agra greatly mortified.[1]

A. H. 1009—A. D. 1600.

When Sultan Sileem returned to Allahabad, he lavishly bestowed upon his adherents, the provincs, situated on the east side of the Ganges. The Soobah of Bahar was given to Kotebeddeen Kokultash; Allah Beg obtained Sircar Jownpoor; and Tunnem Bahadre Sircar Culpee, all as jageers. Besides thus disposing of those valuable provinces, he seized thirty lakhs of rupees that were in the royal treasury of Bahar.[2]

The affection which Akber still entertained for Sileem, only served to increase his affliction, when he received intelligence of his proceedings. He wrote him a letter, wherein he expatiated upon his ingratitude and threatened him with the divine vengeance, for his undutiful and rebellious conduct. Shereef, the son of Khojeh Abdulsemed, of whom the emperor entertained favourable sentiments, was known to be attached to the prince; and Akber flattered himself that by entrusting the negotiation to his management, matters might yet be accommodated so as to preclude the necessity of proceeding to rigorous measures. Sileem received the letter with every mark of dutiful respect, and was

[1] E. D. VI, 99; A. N. (Text) III, 831; M. J. 13; Khaf. I, 218.
[2] M. J. 13.

so much affected at its contents, that he at first resolved to go to his father and throw himself upon his clemency; but upon reflection, did not think it prudent to expose himself to the effects of his just resentment at that time. He retained in his service the Emperor's messenger Shereef, who from that time became his confidential friend; and the very day that he mounted the throne, he made the traitor, his prime minister.[1]

Akber was so much grieved at his son's behaviour, and alarmed for the peace of the empire, that it became the primary object of his attention, to endeavour to bring back the prince to a proper sense of his duty. He, therefore, quitted his military pursuits in the Dekhan, at the time when his arms were most successful; and leaving the command of the army to the Khankhanan and Sheikh Abulfazel, returned to Agra.[2]

A. H. 1010—A. D. 1601.

Some time after the Emperor's return to Agra, Sultan Sileem resolved to pay him a visit in that capital, and set out accompanied by thirty thousand cavalry. Akber was naturally alarmed when he heard that Sileem was coming with such a force; and Jafer Beg Asof Khan, the dewan, who had always opposed the interest of the prince, was so terrified that he entertained thoughts of destroying himself, and when the prince arrived at Etawah, Asof Khan's jageer, he sent him a present of a very valuable ruby. At this place Sileem received

[1] A.N. III, 831. E.D. VI, 99; M.J. 14; Khaf. I, 220; Maasir. III. 626.
[2] Du Jarric, 182.

a letter from his father, telling him that he could not help entertaining unfavourable suspicions of his pretended visit; that it was not the custom for a subject to visit his king at the head of a powerful army; that if in so doing, he had no other object in view, than the displaying of his magnificence and power, he had already effectually accomplished that purpose; and therefore had nothing to do but disband his troops, and come to court alone: but that if he entertained any doubt of his Majesty's sincerity, and had come thus attended to guard himself from danger, he had better return to Allahabad, and not think of an interview till his mind was entirely freed from apprehension and distrust.[1] Sileem, in his answer, entreated his father to believe, that he had no other wish than to throw himself at his Majesty's feet after so long an absence; but that in obedience to his royal command, he should go back to Allahabad without having enjoyed that happiness, and return whenever it might be the Emperor's pleasure to order him to court.

Whilst Sileem remained at Etawah, he received a second letter from his father, wherein he bestowed upon him in jageer, the subahs of Bengal and Orissa, and directed him to send forces to take possession thereof.[2] The prince did not think it prudent to detach any part of his troops at this juncture: he, however, invented some plausible excuses for the delay in the execution of the order,

[1] Du Jarric, pp. 182-3.

[2] M. J., 15-17; Takmil (E. D. VI, 105); Khaf. I, 221-2; De Laet (Lethbridge) p. 198: Du Jarric (Ch. XIII, p. 113).

and with which the Emperor appeared to be satisfied.

Sileem led back his army, and when he arrived at Allahabad displayed all the insignia of royalty, and conferred titles of honour upon his adherents.[1]

In so critical a juncture, the Emperor wishing to avail himself of the faithful and prudent counsel of Abulfazel, ordered him to repair to Agra with all possible expedition. Sileem was conscious of the enormity of his own conduct: he dreaded the effects of Abulfazel's sage advice, which having been ever directed to the welfare of the empire, and the true interest and dignity of his royal master, might, on the present occasion, have operated so far to the disadvantage of the prince, as to have obstructed his accession to the throne, at the death of his father, who was now far advanced in years; he, therefore, formed the base resolution of having him assassinated.[2]

A. H. 1011—A. D. 1602.

The country of Nersingh Deo[3] lay in the road from the Dekhan to Agra; and as this Rajah was then ranked amongst the lawless and unsubjected chieftains, he was easily prevailed upon by the promise of a considerable reward, to execute the foul murder. Accordingly, when Abulfazel arrived at Berkeh Serai, ten cose from Gualiar, he was attacked by a large body of the Rajah's people. He made a gallant resistance, but was soon over-

[1] De Laet (Lethbridge) 198; Du Jarric, 183; Maclagan, 88-9.

[2] R. B. I, 24-5; M. J. [E. D. V. 442-3]; Price (p. 56) assigns religious motives for the act; Khaf. I. 223; Maasir. I, 122-3, 423; Du Jarric 83.

[3] Bir Singh is the correct name.

powered by numbers, and slain; and Nersingh Deo sent his head to Sileem at Allahabad.[1] Although this affair gave Akber great uneasiness, yet it enabled Sileem to go to court without fear or apprehension; and in a short space of time to convert the doubts and jealousy of his father into confidence and satisfaction; for shortly after this event, Akber sent to Allahabad, Selima Sultana Begum,[2] Sileem's mother, to quiet his apprehensions and prevail upon him to repair to court. The prince advanced two days journey to meet his mother, conducted her to Allahabad with every mark of respect; and, without hesitation, consented to return with her to Agra. When he approached near to Agra, he wrote to his father, that in consequence of his kind permission, he was come to make his humble submissions. He entreated that Meriam Mekany,[3] out of her maternal goodness, would receive him under her immediate protection, and begged that the astrologers might determine the fortunate hour for the interview. The letter was entrusted to Khojeh Doast Mohammed. The Emperor, on receipt of it, repaired to the apartments of Meriam Mekany, who cheerfully undertook to comply with Sileem's request. Akber, in his answer, kindly told Sileem that there was no necessity to consult the astrologers, as for such a meeting every hour must be fortunate.

[1] R. B. I, 25; Price 55-6, The trunk was interred at Antari. Asad Beg. E. D. VI, 156-60; Takmil. E. D. VI, 107; M.J. E.D. VI, 442-4.

[2] Widow of Bairam Khan and cousin of Akbar who married her after Bairam's death, R. B. I, 232. Gulbadan Begum's *Humayun Nama* (Beveridge) 276.81; Khaf I, 276.

[3] Hamida Banu Begum, his grand-mother.

Sileem hereupon hastened to Agra, and at the distance of a day's journey from that city was met by Meriam Mekany, who conducted him to her apartments, and there presented him to the Emperor. The prince flung himself at the feet of his father, who raised him from the ground, and after the most tender and affectionate embraces, led him to the presence chamber.[1] Two days afterwards the Emperor gave him one of his finest elephants, and then taking off his own turban placed it upon the head of the prince, and publicly declared him his successor in the Empire.

Akber now represented to Sultan Sileem, that the former expedition against the Ranna having failed through his means, it behoved him to retrieve his reputation by concluding that war in person. The prince cheerfully acquiesced in all that his father proposed; many of the principal munsebdars were nominated for this service; and proper supplies of every kind ordered to be provided without delay. The prince, after taking an affectionate leave of his father, marched to Futtehpoor, and remained there some days in expectation of receiving the promised supplies; but the officers of Government making no progress therein, he saw plainly that they wished to bring him into disgrace by the failure of the expedition for want of proper support. He freely communicated his sentiments to his father, setting forth that his troops were already considerably in arrears; and

[1] R. B. I, 65; M. J. 18-9; Anfaul Akbar E. D. VI, 247; De Laet (tr. Lethbridge,) p. 199; Hadi. 11-12.

that as the Ranna would doubtless protract the war as much as possible, by taking refuge in his mountains, it would be fruitless to engage in such an expedition without very ample resources; but seeing that the Emperor's officers were not disposed to furnish him with the necessary aids, he humbly entreated permission to pay his respects once more to his Majesty, for the purpose of obtaining leave to return to Allahabad;[1] from whence he would undertake the expedition at his own expense.

The Emperor, upon the receipt of the prince's representation, sent Buhkt-ul-Nessa Begum, his own sister, to tell him that he had permission to return to Allahabad, but that having taken his leave in a fortunate hour, the astrologers foretold that another meeting, during the present conjunction of the planets, would be attended with ill consequences: however, that after having stayed a short time at Allahabad, he might return again to Agra.[2] The prince accordingly marched from Futtehpoor, and crossing the Jumna at Mehtra, proceeded to Allahabad: and on his arrival there, he made great rejoicings for the reconciliation that had so happily taken place between him and his father.

The death of Khusru's mother happened about this time. She inherited a melancholy disposition from her family: and the undutiful behaviour of her son,[3] in making use of every opportunity to

[1] Khaf. I, 225-6; M.J. 20-1.
[2] Takmil (E-D.VI, 110); Khaf, 225-6; Maclagan, 91-2.
[3] Terry, p. 411.

prejudice Akber against his father, so worked upon her imagination that taking the opportunity of her husband's absence upon an hunting party she destroyed herself[1] by a large dose of opium. Sileem was a long time inconsolable for the loss of this amiable princess, who, besides a large share of beauty, possessed a fine understanding, with a most engaging softness and affability of manners. Akber sincerely partook of his sorrow, and wrote him a very affectionate and consolatory letter[2] on the occasion.

Although the Emperor had seemingly acquiesced in Sileem's arguments for returning to Allahabad, yet was he by no means satisfied with this pretext for delaying the expedition against the Ranna: and the prince's enemies made use of the occasion to rekindle the Emperor's jealousy, by ascribing this conduct to ambitious designs against the peace of the empire. To add to the Emperor's displeasure Sileem had unhappily, at this time, been guilty of an act of cruelty, which furnished but too just grounds of complaint against him. A wakianavess, or intelligencer, and two other servants belonging to Sileem, had formed a conspiracy against his life; in which being detected, they attempted to make their escape to Sultan Daniel, in the Dekhan; but their flight was soon discovered, and some horsemen being sent in pursuit of them, quickly brought them back. Sileem was so exasperated against them, that in the fury

[1] R. B. I, 55-6; Takmil. E. D. VI, p. 112; M. U. I., 405.
[2] R. B. I, 55-6; Takmil. E. D. VI, p. 112.

of his passion he ordered the wakianavess to be flead, one of the accomplices to be castrated and the other severely beaten. These cruel punishments which were executed in his presence, put an end to the conspiracy; neither were there any more desertions. This transaction, in itself sufficiently culpable, was reported to the Emperor with all the exaggeration that malice could invent. The criminals were represented as innocent sufferers; and it was asserted that the prince commonly practised such barbarities in the paroxisms of inebriation, a vice to which in common with his two brothers, he was unfortunately very much addicted. Akber, who possessed a mind fraught with every principle of philanthropy and humanity, was shocked at these accounts of his son's barbarity. He wrote him a letter, in which he severely reprobated his conduct, and said that not being able himself to see a sheep stripped of its skin without sensations of horror, he was at a loss to conceive how it was possible for his son, so far to stifle the common feelings of nature, as to suffer a fellow creature to be flead in his presence.[1]

A. H. 1012—A. D. 1603.

The Emperor now resolved to go himself to Allahabad, to compel Sileem to come to Agra. He accordingly sent on his tents to the distance of three cose; and at night, unattended, got into a boat in order to proceed thither; but in the middle of the way, the boat struck upon a sand and was immovable. At daybreak some of the nobility

[1] Takmil. E.D. VI, pp. 112-3.

arrived in their boats to his relief; but the astrologers thought this accident a bad omen and recommended to Akbar to return to Agra; he, however, rejected their advice, and proceeded to the encampment. The next day it rained very hard, and he received intelligence that Meriam Mekany, who had always been averse to this journey, was taken ill. The rain continuing with incessant violence for two days, the whole encampment was inundated, and, excepting the royal pavilion, not a tent was left standing. The third night a messenger arrived to inform him that the physicians despaired of his mother's life; upon which he hastened back, in hopes of receiving the last blessing from his beloved parent. But he found her speechless, in which state she continued five days longer, and then expired. The Emperor, according to the custom of his ancestors, shaved his head and beard, and put on a mourning habit; and his example was followed by thousands of all ranks. He assisted in carrying the corpse some paces, after which he returned to the presence chamber. The nobility by turns bore the body to Delhi, where they arrived in thirty-one hours. The body was deposited in the mausoleum of Hemayun. The day after the funeral, the Emperor and his court laid aside their mourning habits; and he bestowed dresses and other valuable presents upon the nobility and the officers of his household.[1]

As soon as Sultan Sileem heard of his father's

[1] Takmil. E.D. VI, p. 113; M. J. P. 22; Khaf. I, 228-30; Du Jarric, 188.

intention to come to Allahabad, and that he had been prevented by the death of Meriam Mekany, he dispatched Shereef to the Subah of Bahar and set out immediately for Agra; to strive to remove the prejudices which the Emperor had conceived against him, as well as to partake of his sorrow for the death of the Begum. His father received him with open arms; and his enemies began to be apprehensive for their safety, from this sudden and unexpected reconciliation. When the court broke up, Akber conducted Sileem to the seraglio. Here the Emperor gave full vent to his rage, and after reprimanding the prince in the severest terms for his misconduct, told him that having heard his brain was turned from his excessive drunkenness, he must remain there some days, in order that, if the report proved true, a proper remedy might be applied to his distemper. He was confined in the oratory, but his mother and sisters were allowed to visit him; and they encouraged him to submit patiently to this treatment, by assuring him that it would terminate to his advantage. He remained there ten days,[1] during which time he entirely abstained from liquor and opium; and behaved in every respect so much to the Emperor's satisfaction that thenceforward he was permitted to come to court and restored to that degree of favour and affection which he had before possessed.

A. H. 1013—A. D. 1604.

But an accident which happened a few days

[1] The authorities differ as regards the exact number of days. Ten is the number to which the most reliable of them incline. Du Jarric, 189.

after Sileem's enlargement was near creating a fresh misunderstanding between him and the Emperor. Sileem was possessed of a very famous elephant named *Geeranbar*, who was an over-match for any one in the royal stables; but Khusru had an elephant named *Aproop*, which he was desirous should enter the lists against his father's. Akber gave orders for the fight, and, according to the custom, one of the royal elephants was directed to be ready on the spot, to assist against the conqueror. Sileem, and his son Khusru, obtained the Emperor's permission to mount their horses, in order to be near the elephants; while the young prince Khorum (afterwards Shahjehan) was seated at a window by the side of his grandfather. The combat began; Khusru's elephant soon gave way, and the Emperor's was pushing forward to support him against the conqueror; but a number of people for some time refused to let the royal elephant pass before Sileem's horse, and flung stones, one of which cut the Emperor's elephant driver on the side of his head and some blood issued from the wound; however, he pressed on, and at length brought his elephant into action. The insidious Khusru galloped away to the Emperor, and told him that the disturbance had been occasioned by his father, who had secretly given directions to his people not to suffer the royal elephant to engage. The Emperor sent young Khorum to tell his father how much he was displeased at him and to desire to know what had induced him to behave in such an extraordinary manner. Khorum delivered the

Emperor's message in the most respectful terms, and Sileem desired him to assure the Emperor, that so far from conniving at, he had actually quelled the disturbance. By this time Khusru's elephant had run away, and Sileem's gained such superiority over the imperial one, that his life was in danger. All attempts to part them proved in vain, till at length they plunged together into the river, where they were separated by the interposition of some people in boats: Khorum returned to his grandfather, and proved to his satisfaction the falsity of Khusru's accusation.[1]

On Monday the 20th of Jemady ul Awwel, A. H. 1014, or 13th August 1605, Akber was seized with a fever,[2] the violence of which greatly alarmed his physicians. At this juncture Sileem received secret intelligence that a party, at the head of which were Mansingh, Khusru's uncle, and Khan Azem, his father-in-law, had formed a design of raising Khusru to the throne, upon the death of the Emperor: he therefore did not think it prudent to put himself in the power of the conspirators by venturing into the fort of Agra to visit his father.[3] But young Khorum could not be prevailed upon to leave the Emperor for a moment, although his mother went on purpose to bring him away, and remonstrated with him on the danger to which he exposed himself, by remaining amongst his

[1] Asad Beg E. D. VI, pp. 168-9.

[2] Price, 122-4.

[3] [illegible] 124-5, 125-35, gives an account differing essentially from that found in R. B. Tod's Rajasthan (Routledge) II, pp. 286-7 gives an incorrect account; Asad Beg, E. D. VI, pp. 169-70; Maasir I, 327; De Laet (Calcutta Review) I-II, 1871, p. 77.

enemies; all entreaties were in vain, and he declared that no consideration should separate him from his beloved grandfather, as long as there remained in him any signs of life.

At length the conspirators, finding themselves discovered, began to entertain doubts of their success; and after some debate they agreed that it would be most prudent to lay aside their design till a more favourable opportunity. They accordingly waited upon Sileem, and swore to act in obedience to his authority. The next day he visited the Emperor in his last moments.[1]

On the night of the 13th of Jemady-ul-Sany, or October 13th, 1605, Akber expired, and the next day was interred with great pomp in the cemetery at Secundra. He was born in A. H. 949, or A. D. 1542; ascended the throne in 963, or A. D. 1556, at the age of fourteen, and died after a glorious reign of forty-nine solar years; aged sixty-three solar years and one day.[2]

He had three sons, Sultan Sileem, now Jehangir; Sultan Morad, who died by excessive drinking in A. H. 1007, or A. D. 1598, in the Dekhan; and Sultan Daniel, who died by the like debauch also in the Dekhan, in A. H. 1013, or A. D. 1604: and three daughters Shahzadeh Khanun; Sheker-ul-Nissa Begum; and Aram Banu Begum.

[1] Price, pp. 125-35.

[2] Takmil, E. D. VI, p. 115; Asad Beg E. D. VI, pp. 170-2; Du Jarric, 203-5; M. J. 29; Khaf. I, 235; Du Jarric and Bartoli (Mr. V. A. Smith's Akbar, p. 326), assert that Akbar died of poison. *See* also Tod I, 279, and II, [illegible]; Terry, 408-9; Herbert, p. 72, Peter Mundy II, 102-3.

THE

HISTORY OF HINDOSTAN.

VOL. I.

JEHANGIR.

On Thursday, the 20th of Jemady-ul-Sany, A. H. 1014, corresponding with the 22nd of October, A. D. 1605,[1] Sultan Sileem ascended the throne at Agra, and assumed the following titles: *Abulmozuffer Noureddeen Mohammed Jehangir*, or *the Father of Victory, the Light of Religion, Mohammed, the Conqueror of the World.*

He tells us, in his own memoirs, that the first order he issued, on his accession to the throne, was for the construction of the golden chain of justice,[2] which we shall describe particularly amongst his other regulations. He confirmed all the laws that had been enacted by his father, and issued an edict containing twelve institutes,[3] or regulations, remarkable for the humanity, justice, and political sagacity that pervade them, and which we shall detail in the proper place.

A. H. 1014—A. D. 1605.

The following appointments and promotions[4] immediately took place:—On Syeed Khan,[5] one

[1] According to R. B. I, p. 5, 24th October, 1605; Price, gives p. 2, 10th October, 1605. Jahangir was 37 years 3 months old at the time according to the Lunar calendar and 36 years and 1 month by Solar reckoning. His accession was on the eighth day after Akbar's death. Du Jarric. III, xvi.

[2] [illegible]ice, p. 8.

[3] Price, p. 8; R. B. I, 7-10; 15.

[4] R. B. I, 13-16; 18.

[5] Price, p. 26.

of Akber's confidential omrahs, was conferred the Government of the Punjab ; Sheikh Fereed Bokharee,[1] the late Emperor's Meer Bukhshee*, was confirmed in his office ; Mokeem, to whom Akber, in the latter end of his reign, had given the title of Vizier Khan,[2] was now appointed to the office of Vizier ul Memalek* jointly with Jan Beg, to whom Jehangir, before he came to the throne, had given the title of Vizier ul Mulk **: Rajah Mansingh was appointed Subahdar of Bengal : Khojehgee Futtehullah, Abdulrezak Mamoory, both Bukshees, or Paymasters, and Ameenneddeen, all officers of the late Emperor, were confirmed in their respective posts ; and all the inferior public servants, with those of the harem, continued to enjoy their accustomed stipends. Shereef Khan,[3] who had been appointed Subahdar of Bahar, during the time of Akber, was now promoted to the high dignities of Vakeel ul Sultanet***, and Ameer ul Omrah.**** Khan Azem was retained about the Emperor's person, with every mark of confidence and respect.

The Ranna of Oudypoor, having shaken off the yoke upon the death of Akber, Jehangir, in order to reduce him to obedience, sent against him his second son, Sultan Purveiz, with an army of twenty

[1] Price, p. 29.

* Paymaster-General.

[2] Price 49-50.

*Grand Vizier : during the reign of Jehangir, this office was generally executed by two persons jointly.

**Vizier of the Empire.

[3] Price, 30.

***For a particular account of the office of *Vakeel ul Sultanet*, see the preface to the English Translation of the Ayeen Akbery, Vol. I, page iv, quarto edition.

****The prince of princes.

thousand cavalry;[1] but the prince, being only sixteen years of age, the actual command was entrusted to Asof Khan, in the quality of Ataleek, or Tutor.[2] When they took their leave of Jehangir, he charged them, that if either the Ranna or his son Kurrun came out to meet them with tokens of submission, they should receive him kindly, and not commit any hostility upon the country.[3] The Emperor was actuated to this moderate conduct by two motives. The vast territory of Mawerelnehr* being at this time in great confusion without a head; and the Dekhan having been but partly subdued by Akber, he was tempted to look to the conquest of the former kingdom, and to the finishing, in the latter quarter, what his father had begun. But whilst so powerful a prince as the Ranna of Oudypoor continued unsubdued, it would have been highly imprudent to have engaged himself in foreign expeditions.

In the first month of his reign, Jehangir had, by one of his concubines, male twins, whom he called Jehandar and Sheriar.[4]

Lallah Beg Behadre,[5] who had shewn a faithful attachment to the Emperor in the lifetime of his father, he now promoted to a munseb of 4000, gave him a present of 20,000 rupees, and appointed him Soobahdar of Bahar. At the same time Vizier Khan was appointed Dewan** of Bengal.

[1] R.B. I, 16; Iqbal, 7; M.J., p. 36; Khaf. I, 249.
[2] Price 54-5; For his life see M. J. I. 282-7.
[3] [illegible]B, I, 26.
* The country beyond the river Jihoon or Oxus; Transoxonia.
[4] Price 35, gives a wrong description R. B. I, 20.
[5] Price 40-1; R. B. I, 21.
**The Superintendent of the collection of the revenues.

Rajah Nersingh Deo[1], who, at the instigation of Jehangir, had put to death, the great Abulfazel, was in the first year of his reign promoted to a munseb of 3000.

A. H. 1014—A. D. 1606.

Jehangir had reigned only six months, when his eldest son, Sultan Khusru,[2] appeared in open rebellion against him. It has already been mentioned that during Akber's last illness, Rajah Mansingh,[3] Khusru's maternal uncle, and Azem Khan his father-in-law, in conjunction with others of the Omrahs, who, from having always opposed the interest of Sultan Sileem, dreaded that when he came to the throne, they should become the victims of his resentment, instilled ambitious notions into the mind of young Khusru, which led him to form the resolution of disputing the crown with his father; when a favourable opportunity should offer; and which they persuaded him was not then far distant, as the nobility in general were caballing, in order to be ready to take advantage of the confusion that might naturally be looked for at the death of Akber.[4] But the unexpected reconciliation which fortunately took place between the Emperor and Sultan Sileem, dissolved the conspiracy and put him in quiet possession of the Empire.[5] The rebellious designs of Khusru, and his party, being thereby

[1] He was Bir Singh, generally styled Narsingh by the Persian Chronicles R.B. I, 24-5.

[2] Roe, 247, 256, 289, 299.

[3] See R. B. I, 138 for Jahangir's opinion of Raja Man Singh.

[4] Asad Beg, E. D. VI 169-70, Price, 124-5.

[5] Asad Bag, E. D. VI, 170-2.

frustrated, he was observed to be uncommonly melancholy, and thoughtful, as if meditating some desperate enterprise; and all his father's endeavours to gain his confidence and affection, by every act of royal favour and paternal indulgence,[1] had no effect upon him. He continued in this state till the 8th of the month Zilhejeh, or April 8th, 1606; when, at night, under pretence of visiting the tomb of his grandfather, Akber, he departed from the fort of Agra, with about an hundred and fifty horsemen. His flight was immediately discovered to Jan Beg, the Vizier, by one of his link-boys, who happened to be known to that minister.[2] The Vizier, without loss of time, carried the man to the Ameer ul Omrah, who after examining him, and being convinced of the truth of his report from the consistency of his story, ran alone to the palace, and calling out one of the eunuchs of the Serai* desired him to present his duty to his Majesty, and inform him, that he had some very important intelligence, which required instant communication. Jehangir, from whose memoirs we have taken this account,[3] says, he had no conception of what had really happened; but imagined that some intelligence had arrived either from the Dekhan or Gujerat. When the Ameer ul Omrah had disclosed the matter to him, they consulted together on the measures most proper to be taken. The Emperor

[1] R. B. I, 12. A lakh of rupees was given to him for the repair of Munim Khan's Mansion at Agra to be used as his residence. Price p. 26. Jahangir says h[illegible] constrained to imprison Khusru in the upper part of the royal tower in the castle of Agra from which he should have escaped.

[2] Price p. 113.

* The women's apartments and seraglio.

[3] R. B. I, 51-70.

proposed that either himself, or Sultan Khorum, his third son, should go in pursuit of the fugitive: to both of which proposals the Ameer ul Omrah started objections, and offered his own services, which were accordingly accepted. He asked his Majesty what course he was to take, provided the prince should refuse to listen to reason. The Emperor answered that if Khusru did not peaceably surrender himself, the Ameer ul Omrah should not be responsible for any measures that he might think it advisable to pursue, adding the following political maxim: "That when the peace of an empire is at stake, no regard must be paid even to our children, for that a King has no relations". The Ameer ul Omrah took his leave; but after some further consideration, the Emperor, reflecting upon the inveterate hatred which the Prince bore towards this minister, did not choose to expose him to the effects of his resentment, in case, through any misfortune, he should fall into his hands. He, therefore, ordered him back, and sent in his stead Sheikh Fareed Bokharee with such a body of troops as he could hastily collect, accompanied by Ehtemam Khan, the Cutwal*. His Majesty resolved to follow the next morning, at the head of a considerable force.[1]

Ahamed Beg Khan, and Doast Mohammed who had that day taken their leave of his Majesty to visit their native country, happened to be at Secundra, when Khusru arrived there, and they

* Superintendent of the Police.

[1] Price 116-7 mentions 40,000 horses and 100,000 camels as having been brought out and distributed amongst the soldiers and armies.

hastening back to Agra, confirmed the other man's report, with the additional information, that Khusru intended to proceed to Penjab. The Emperor suspected that he would soon quit that road, and retire to Bengal, to Rajah Mansingh, the Soobahdar, who was his maternal uncle; but it was soon afterwards ascertained that he had actually pursued the way to Penjab.

When Khusru arrived at Mehtra, he met with Hassan Beg Bedakhshee, on his way to Agra from Cabul from which Government he had lately been dismissed. Khusru easily persuaded him to join his party with about three hundred men, and return with him to Penjab. They attacked and plundered every one who fell in their way, and seized some horses, upon which they mounted their infantry; even women and children did not escape their fury; and they burnt all the villages through which they passed. Khusru was much affected at beholding these scenes of violence and distress, but was obliged to comply with what he had not the power to prevent.[1] At the same time that he reached Paniput, Dilawer Khan, Governor of Lahoor, happened to arrive there also, on his way to that city; and hearing of the rebellion, sent his women and children across the river Jumnah, that, returning alone by forced marches, he might be able to reach Lahoor before Khusru. Near Paniput, he met with Abdulraheem, whom he advised to send his family also on the other side of the Jumnah, and to wait there himself until the

[1] Price 220-1.

Emperor arrived. Dilawer Khan set out immediately for Lahoor and alarmed all the country through which he passed with his account of Khusru's rebellion, and of the devastations committed by his followers. Some he engaged to join him, and others were persuaded to continue neuter. No sooner was Dilawer Khan departed, than Abdulraheem acted in direct contradiction to his advice, and joined Khusru, who gave him the title of Mallick ul Vuzeerah, or, The Prince of Viziers.[1]

At day-break, the Emperor began his march. When he arrived at Secundra, he made his offerings at his father's shrine and then proceeded on his way. Here Mirza Hussein, one of the sons of Mirza Sharokh, who had been one of the companions of Khusru's flight, having lost his way in the night, was surprised and taken. Not being able to deny the fact, he was tied hand and foot and put upon an elephant.[2] The sun being intensely powerful, the Emperor was obliged to halt, during the heat of the day, under the shade of some trees. He went on again in the afternoon, and at night encamped by the side of a tank in the pergunnah of Mehtra, about twenty-three cose distant from Agra. On the 10th he marched to Hodal.[3] From this place he sent forward a choice body of men, commanded by Sheikh-Fereed Bokharee. On the 11th the Emperor marched to Palwal; and on the 12th to Feredabad. On the 13th he arrived at

[1] Price 141. R. B. I, 59.
[2] R. B. I, 58.
[3] Manucci I, 71.

Delhi where he paid his devotions at the tomb of Hemayun; on the 14th he arrived at Nereyleh Serai, which place, Khusru in his march, had burnt down. The 15th he halted. The 16th he marched to Paniput. The 17th he marched to Kernal; halted on the 18th, and on the 19th proceeded to Shahabad, where he halted some days. Dilawer Khan having thrown himself into Lahoor, with a considerable reinforcement, was very active in putting that place in a posture of defence, in which he was cheerfully assisted by all the garrison as well as the inhabitants of the city.[1] Two days after his arrival, Khusru besieged the place and promised his men, that they should have the plundering of the city for seven days.[2] The besiegers set fire to one of the city gates, but the active Dilawer Khan stopped their progress, by building up a wall withinside. The same day Sayeed Khan, with a body of troops from Cashmeer, happening to encamp on the banks of the Chenab, where he heard of the rebellion, hastened to the relief of Lahoor; and at night he and his party were received into the fort.[3]

When Khusru had laid before Lahoor six days, he received intelligence that the imperial army was advancing against him.[4] By this time, he had been joined by many of the inhabitants of Lahoor, which is one of the most populous cities of Hindoostan, so that he found himself at the

[1] Price 140.
[2] Price 147, R. B. I, 62.
[3] R. B. I, 62, Iqbal 10, 11, Khaf. I, 251.
[4] R. B. I, 62.

head of ten or twelve thousand cavalry. He, therefore, thought it most advisable to raise the siege, and march to attack the Emperor's advanced guard, under the command of Sheikh Fareed, who was encamped at Sultanpoor. Although it was night and rained violently, when the Emperor received advice of Khusru's motions, he marched instantly, and arrived the next morning at Sultanpoor, on the river Bias, where he remained till noon. Nobody having suspected that a battle could possibly be fought that day, the Imperial troops, according to the custom of eastern armies, had come on in small parties, without observing any order in their march, and the Emperor was just sitting down to take a slight repast,[1] when news was brought him that Khusru had attacked Sheikh Fereed, and the advanced body. He mounted his horse and flew to the army, attended only by fifty horsemen. By the time he reached the bridge of Govindwal, he had collected together about five hundred men; but here he learnt that the enemy were totally routed.[2] The news was brought him by Shumsee Towshekehee, to whom he instantly gave the title of Khooshkubber Khan*. Sheikh Fereed gained great honour by this victory. Sief Khan, of the tribe of Bareh, who fought under Fereed received seventeen wounds. The band of this tribe, who were not above sixty in number, cut to pieces[3] a great many

1 Price 149.
2 For account of battle see price 151.
* The Khan, or Lord, who brings glad tidings.
3 R.B. I, 64 says that 'the Sayyids of Barha having received wounds from 1500 Badakshani horsemen had been cut to pieces.'

of the Bedakshian cavalry* As soon as they perceived them giving way, they cried out GOD SAVE THE EMPEROR when the rebels imagining Jehangir was actually arrived, fled with the utmost precipitation. A box of jewels, and other things of great value, belonging to Khusru, were left on the field of battle.[1]

The very night that Khusru fled from Agra, the Emperor had dispatched Rajah Bassoo to his Zemindary in the mountains of Lahoor, with orders to seize Khusru if he appeared in that quarter; and at the same time Mehabut Khan, and Mirza Aly Akber were sent with a body of troops, to follow him wherever they could hear of him.

On the 28th of Zilhejeh, or 26th April, the imperial army encamped at Chaul,[2] seven cose from Lahoor. After the battle of Govindwal, the forces of Khusru dispersed, so that he was left only with a few Afghans, who had been long in his service; and Hassan Beg's party which was now very inconsiderable. The Afghans advised him to return to Agra and create disburbances in that quarter; but Hassan Beg having left his family and treasure at Cabul, pressed him to repair thither. This advice he, unfortunately for himself, embraced, when all the Afghans deserted him. In the night, after the battle, Khusru, Abdulraheem and Hassan Beg, with a small party, arrived on the Banks of the Chenab, intending to

* According to the Masir Jehangiry, the incredible—' Padshah Salamat ' long live the King.

[1] The box fell into the hands of some persons who, according to Price p. 15, were never discovered.

[2] Elliot VI. 299 calls it ' Jahan '

have crossed over at the ferry of Shahpoor; but not finding a boat there, they proceeded to Soodra. Here were lying two boats, one empty and without men, and the other loaded with firewood and straw. They forced the people out of the loaded boat, into the empty one, but neither promises nor threats could engage them to use their oars. Immediately upon the defeat of Khusru's army, orders had been issued to the guards at all the ferries in Penjab, not to suffer any person to pass unexamined; and the watermen were afraid to offend against so positive an order at such a critical time. The Chowdry* of Soodra, hearing a violent noise at the ferry, hastened thither, and found that some persons wanted to cross over although it was night. He therefore called out to them to stop, as it was the Emperor's positive command, that no person should pass the river, who could not give a good account of himself. The noise raised the neighbourhood, and both sides of the river were soon lined with people. The Chowdry took off the rudder of the boat, and Hassan Beg having forced it from the shore, it drove down with the stream till day break, when its progress was stopped by a sand upon which it stuck so fast, that all efforts to get it off were in vain. Abul Cossim and Khojeh Khyzir Khan, by order of Hillal Khan, had now possessed themselves of the western bank of the river, and the east side was defended by the zemindars. This Hillal Khan, just before the rebellion broke out, had been ordered to join

* inferior Zemindar.

the army of Saiyeed Khan, in Cashmeer, and arrived here at this juncture on his way to that Subah. Khusru's party let fly some arrows; but such feeble resistance answered no purpose ; men, mounted on elephants plunged into the river, and being joined by others in boats, the Prince and his party were easily made prisoners.[1]

A. H. 1015—A. D. 1606.

The next morning Khusru was brought before his father, with a chain fastened from his left hand to his left foot, according to the laws of Chenghez Khan. On the right hand of the Prince stood Hassan Beg and on his left Abdulraheem. Khusru trembled and wept. He was ordered into confinement; but the companions of his rebellion were put to death with cruel torments. Hassan Beg was sewed up in the raw hide of an ox, and Abdulraheem in that of an ass, and both were led about the town on asses, with their faces towards the tail.[2] The ox's hide became so dry and contracted, that before the evening Hassan Beg was suffocated: but the ass's hide being continually moistened with water, by the friends of Abdulraheem, he survived the punishment, and afterwards obtained the Emperor's pardon. From the garden of Kamran to the city of Lahoor, two rows of stakes were fixed in the ground, upon which the other rebels were impaled alive ;[3] and the unhappy Khusru, mounted on an elephant, was conducted

[1] Price gives a different account of the way in which Khusru fell into the hands of the Imperialists, p. 151.

[2] Du Jarric gives a detailed account of the punishment.

[3] Price 153.

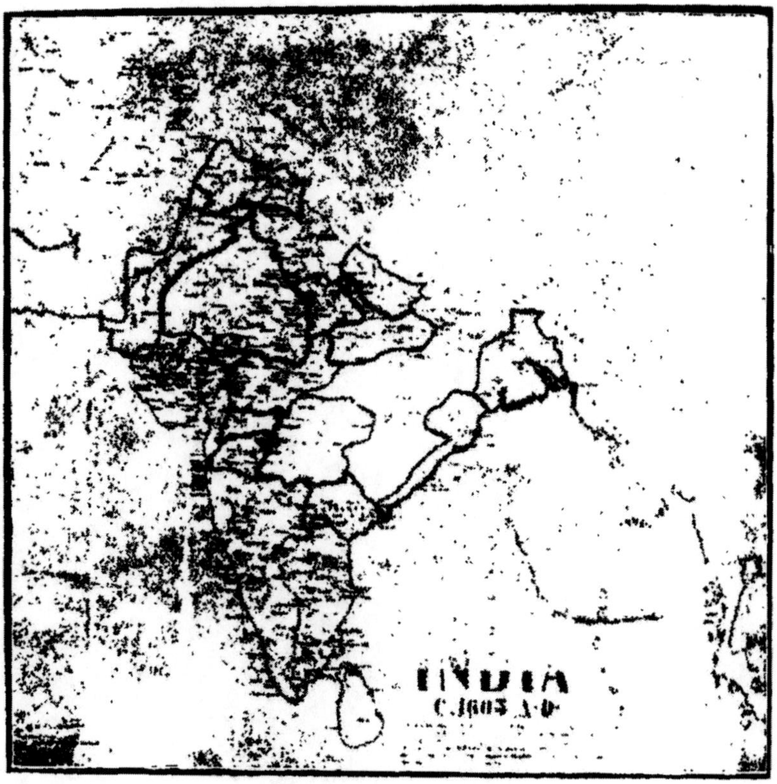

JAHANGIR'S INDIA

between the ranks of these miserable sufferers.[1]

The Emperor honoured Sheikh Fereed with the title of Mortiza Khan; and the zemindars who had shown their loyalty, during the insurrection, were rewarded by a grant of Seyurghal*, of all the country situated between the rivers Biah and Chenab.

In order to protect Agra, and prevent further insurrections, the Emperor, at the time he marched against Sultan Khusru, had sent orders for Sultan Purveiz, and Asof Khan to repair to that quarter with part of the army; leaving the rest employed against the Ranna. Fortunately, before Purveiz received these orders, he had concluded a peace with the Ranna; who had sent to the Prince one of his relations, named Nagh, to make his submission to the Emperor.[2] Khusru's rebellion was so suddenly quashed, that Purveiz had not time to reach Agra, before he received fresh orders from his father to repair to Lahoor.

The Jageerdars of the provinces of Ferah and Seistan, headed by the Governor of Herat, on the part of Shah Abbass, King of Persia, thinking the death of Akber and Khusru's rebellion, favourable conjunctures for such an enterprise, laid siege to the fortress of Kandahar. Shah Beg Khan, the Governor, after strengthening the fortification. defended the place with an intrepidity bordering upon rashness; exposing himself to the view of

1 Gladwin makes no mention of the sad fate of the Sikh Guru Arjun Singh who was put to death for the favour he had shown to Khusru at the time of his rebellion.

* For a description of this kind of grant, vide Ayeen Akbari, vol. I, p. 280.

2 R. B. I. 74. A truce was concluded near Mandalgarh.

the besiegers from the upper works, where he sat drinking and carousing, as if it had been a time of perfect peace and security. He made several gallant sallies, and cut to pieces a considerable number of the assailants, who were making preparations for converting the siege into a blockade. As soon as the Emperor received intelligence of these transactions, he sent a large reinforcement to the relief of the place under the command of Mirza Ghazi, accompanied by Sirdar Khan, and other officers of high rank. The Emperor could not help admiring the intrepidity of Shah Beg Khan; but, did not, however, think it advisable to continue in the command of so important a fortress, one, whose conduct was at the same time so rash and inconsiderate; he was, therefore, removed to the Subahdary of Cabul, and Sirdar Khan appointed in his stead Governor of Kandahar. When the army of Mirza Ghazi arrived within six days march of Kandahar, the enemy raised the siege and dispersed to their respective habitations.[1]

Shah Abbass seeing the ill success of the enterprise, thought it most prudent to disclaim it; and accordingly wrote, in angry terms, to Hussein Khan the Beglerbegy of Khorasan &c. and commanded him to withdraw his forces from the siege. This letter was sent by Hussein Beg, who had directions, after having settled the commotions in those parts, to proceed to Jehangir and assure him of the King of Persia's entire ignorance of the plot, and high indignation against the perpetra-

[1] R. B. I., 70-1; 85-6.

tors of so scandalous an outrage. Hussein Beg waited upon Jehangir, at Lahoor, who also, thinking it most prudent to dissemble upon the occasion, gave the Persian Ambassador a very honourable reception.[1] Sirdar Khan was soon after removed, when the joint government of Kandahar and Tatah was conferred upon Mirza Ghazi.

About this time Sultan Purveiz, and Asof Khan, arrived at Lahoor ; the former was raised to the command of ten thousand cavalry, with the ensign of the Aftabgeer*; the latter also met with a very gracious reception.

Mocurreb Khan at this time brought from Burhanpoor, the children of the deceased Sultan Daniel, three sons, Tehmuras, Baisanker and Housheng ; and three daughters, who were received by the Emperor with parental affection.

As soon as the rebellion was quelled, the Emperor sent orders for Miriam-ul-Zemanee, his own mother, and Rokiah Sultana Begum, another of Akber's widows, together with his own wives, and the young Prince Sultan Khorum, to repair to Lahoor.

There was now an insurrection at Nagore, headed by Roysingh and his son Dowleb ; which was quelled by the exertions of Rajah Juggernaut and the Imperial troops stationed in Ajmeer.

On the Solar anniversary of the Emperor's birthday, when he entered into the thirty-eighth-

[1] R. B. I., 85-6; 90 ; 112.

* A kind of umbrella, an ensign of royalty.

year of his age, he was weighed in the apartments of Miriam-ul-Zemanee,[1] with the usual ceremonies, eleven [2] times; the first time against gold, and the other ten against silver, and other metals, perfumes, exhilarating drugs &c. This ceremony of weighing the Emperor of Hindostan, is performed twice in every year, on the solar, and on the lunar anniversary of his birth; and the gold and other articles are bestowed in charity. During this festival, Kotebeddeen Koka, whose mother had suckled the Emperor, and whom he loved with a brotherly affection, was appointed Subahdar of Bengal and Orissa, in the room of Rajah Mansingh, who was ordered to repair to court. Kotebeddeen was on this occasion promoted to the rank of five thousand cavalry; and Jehangir ordered two lakhs of rupees to be issued from the treasury for his particular use, and three lakhs for the payment of his army.

The nuptials of Sultan Purveiz with the daughter of his deceased uncle Sultan Morad, were now celebrated with great magnificence. The Emperor bestowed upon the princess a present of one lakh and fifty thousand rupees; besides a lakh of rupees for his son's expenses.

Shahbaz Bahadre Kulmac, who had been a long time in open rebellion in Bengal, now made his submission to the Emperor, who readily received him into favour, bestowed upon him a Khunjer *

[1] Maryam-Zamani.

[2] Twelve times according to the Tazuk [R. B. I., 78].

* A short sword. The learned Sir William Jones has observed in one of his discourses addressed to the R. Asiatic Society, that Hanger is a corruption of Khenje.

inlaid with precious stones and eight thousand rupees in money, and promoted him to the command of a thousand cavalry.

After the celebration of the nuptials, the Emperor made an excursion to Goorjhakundeneh, one of the royal hunting seats in Penjab; leaving Khusru at Lahoor under the charge of Asof Khan. He was absent from Lahoor about three months.

Sungram, a powerful and rebellious zemindar of Bahar, was defeated and killed by Lalla Bazbahadre, who, in reward for this service, was made a munsebdar of ten thousand,[1] with the title of Jehangeer Kuly Khan; and shortly afterwards obtained the Subahdary of Bahar.

About this time, died at Lahoor, the mother of Kotebeddeen Kokultash.* She had given suck to the Emperor, and he had always behaved towards her with the same respect as if she had been his mother. He assisted in carrying her corpse some part of the way to the grave, and was so afflicted for the loss of her, that he refused food, and would not change his clothes for several days.[2]

The Emperor now thought proper to declare Sultan Khorum his heir; his munseb was increased to eight thousand zat, and five thousand cavalry of two and three horses; he was allowed to make use of the red seraperdah,** a mark of distinction

[1] Jahangir (R. B. I., 82-3) says he was promoted to the rank of 4,500 personal and 3,500 horse in March 1617.

* Kokultash, in the Turkish language, signifies, foster mother.

[2] R. B. I., 84-5.

** None but the Imperial tents are covered with red cloth, without a special permission from the Emperor.

heretofore peculiar to the Emperor, and Sircar Hissar was given him in Jageer.[1]

When Baber began the conquest of Hindostan, the first Jageer which he granted was Sircar Hissar to his son Hemayun. On Hemayun's accession to the throne, he bestowed this place in like manner upon Akber, who, when he came to the empire, gave it to Jehangir; and he, in imitation of his ancestors, conferred it upon the heir apparent. The royal signet called Ouzek * was committed to the care of Sultan Khorum, and it was commanded, that in all grants and patents he should be recognised heir apparent.

Abdullah Khan, Governor of Culpee, brought in chains to the Emperor, Rajah Ramchund, the rebellious Zemindar of Bundeyleh. Prince Khorum entreated for his pardon, and had the pleasure of taking off his chains, and of obtaining for him a Khelut.[2] He was given in charge to Rajah Bassoo with orders to exact security for his future good conduct and then to set him at liberty. Abdullah Khan was immediately rewarded with a munseb of four thousand, with other marks of royal favour, and after a short attendance at court, he obtained in marriage the daughter of Mirza Soliman, Governor of Bedakshan, a descendant of Abusyed Mirza, and Sircar Sironje in Malwah, was granted to him in Jageer.

[1] R. B., 87, 132.

* The impression of the Ouzek Signet is offered to all Fermons vide, Ayeen Akbari, vol. I, p. 67.

[2] Jahangir (R. B, I., 82, 87) makes no mention of Khurm's intercession but claims the credit for himself. Two years later he married Ram Chand's daughter.

A.H. 1016—A.D. 1607.

The Emperor now marched with his army to Cabul, to reduce to obedience the refractory Afghans in that neighbourhood. He left Lahoor on the 7th of Zelhejeh, or 25th March 1607, and arrived at Cabul on the 18th of Sefer or 3rd June 1607.

About this time, Asof Khan was promoted to the High office of the Vekalut[1], in the room of the Ameer-ul-Omrah; on which occasion he presented to his Majesty a ruby, valued at forty thousand rupees. Abdul Hussain was appointed his naib.

A few days after the Emperor's arrival at Cabul, he visited the tomb of Baber, and gave directions for laying out an extensive garden adjoining to that of Shehr Ara, to which he gave the name of Jehan Ara, or, the ornament of the world, and ordered that the river of Cabul should be brought, by a Canal, through this new garden.

He now received intelligence of the death of Aly Kuly Beg Sheer Afkun Khan, and of Kotebed-deen Khan, of which event, the following is a summary account. Aly Kuly Beg Atageelu, had been employed as an Ambassador by Shah Ismail, King of Persia, and upon the death of that monarch, came into Hindostan, where, entering into the service of the Khankhanan, during this expedition in Tatah, he so distinguished himself by his valour and good conduct, that he was rewarded with a considerable munseb, and afterwards married the daughter of Ghias Beg. When Akber marched

[1] *i.e.* the Viziership R. B. I., 103. The Amir-ul-Amara was suffering from a severely incapacitating illness. This Asaf Khan is Qawa-mu-d-din Jafar Beg. He had been made Mir Bakshi by Akbar in 989 A.H. (1581) R. B. I., 106

into the Dekhan, and sent Jehangir, then Sultan Sileem, against the Ranna of Oudypoor, Aly Kuly Beg was left under his command, and behaved so much to his satisfaction, that he then gave him the title of Sheer Afkun, or the "lion's overthrower;" and when he came to the throne, sent him into Bengal with a considerable command. Afterwards, having become restless and refractory, the Emperor told Kotebeddeen, when he was appointed Subahdar of Bengal, to endeavour to reclaim Sheer Afkun by kind treatment, but if that failed, to order him to court, and in case of disobedience, to punish him according to his deserts. Kotebeddeen Khan began with friendly advice and gentle admonition, but without effect, not being even able to prevail upon him to come to an interview; which having reported to Jehangir, he commanded him to proceed to severity. On receipt of this order, Kotebeddeen set out, slightly attended, to Burdwan, where the Jageer of Sheer Afkun was situated, and he hearing that the Subahdar was coming almost alone, met him with only two servants; but Kotebeddeen had placed a number of men in ambush, who rushed out and surrounded Sheer Afkun. Upon this, he drew his sword, and ripped up the belly of Kotebeddeen, when Iybek Khan, who was along with the Subahdar, wounded Sheer Afkun in the head, who nevertheless, deprived Iybek Khan of his life at one stroke. Sheer Afkun was now beset by the whole party, and cut to pieces; Kotebeddeen expired a few hours after. The Emperor was greatly afflicted at the death of

Kotebeddeen, who, as has been already observed, was his foster brother.[1] Jehangir Kuly Khan, Subahdar of Bahar, was appointed Subahdar of Bengal upon the death of Kotebeddeen, and Islam Khan was sent from Agra to Patna, to take charge of that Subah.

The Emperor, whilst he was at Cabul, sent for Sultan Khusru, and ordering his fetters to be taken off, permitted him to walk in the garden of Shere Ara, and seemed every way disposed to receive him again into favour.[2] But on his return to Lahoor, when he arrived at Soorkhab, it was discovered that Khusru had kept up a correspondence with some conspirators, who had resolved to assassinate the Emperor when he was hunting. The plot was discovered by the confession of one of the conspirators, to Khojeh Wiess, Sultan Khorum's Dewan; and a numerous list of his associates was also delivered in. Asof Khan represented to the Emperor that the exercising of violent measures might excite such commotions, as it would be difficult to quell upon a march; and, moreover to prevent further bloodshed, advised him not to be curious in examining the list, but rather to destroy it. This advice appeared so prudent, that only three persons were put to death; after which no further inquisition was made into the affair.[3]

[1] R. B. I. 113-15.

[2] R. B. I. 111, 122-3; Iqbal 27, 28, 29, 30; Du Jarric Ch. XVIII, 160-1.

[3] R. B. 122-3; Du Jarric Chap. XVII, 160-1; Maasir I. 282-3; Iqbal 27-30. Khusru was probably blinded then. For its nature and effects see E. D. VI, 448, 449, 452; Hawkins Voyages p. 428; Finch in Parchas IV, 51; Della Valle (Travels) I, 56; Tavernier I, 334-5.

Hashem Khan was now promoted to the rank of five thousand, and appointed Subahdar of Orissa.

Whilst the army was encamped at Lahoor, Asof Khan made a magnificent entertainment, which his Majesty honoured with his presence. Asof Khan's presents in jewels, stuffs, and elephants were valued at ten lakhs of rupees, a small part of which was accepted.[1]

Mortiza Khan sent the Emperor, from Gujerat, two rubies, valued at twenty-five thousand rupees each; one was considered as a great curiosity, being an entire ring made out of one stone.

The Shereef of Mecca sent to Jehangir an ambassador, with a complimental letter, and a present of one of the curtains of the holy temple. The ambassador received a present of seven thousand rupees, and a lakh of rupees was ordered to be expended in the most curious productions of Hindostan to be sent to the Shereef.[2]

The insurrections in Gujerat and the Dekhan being still unquelled, the Emperor resolved to return to Agra. He marched to Delhy, where he remained four days at Sileemgurh, and celebrated the festival of the new year, at the village of Rungteh,[3] four cose from Delhy.

A. H. 1017—A. D. 1607.

Rajah Mansingh after repeated orders met the Emperor near Agra, and brought him one hundred elephants, but all unserviceable. Notwithstanding

[1] R. B. I. 132.

[2] R. B. I. 133.

[3] R. B. I. 139 says it is 5 Kos. from Agra. The Agra volume of the Imp. Gazett. (p. 764) spells it as Runkutta.

Jehangir was possessed of the fullest proofs of his perfidy, and knew that Khusru had been guided entirely by his evil counsel;[1] yet, in consideration of his powerful interest with the Rajahs of Hindostan, it was judged best to give him a favourable reception.

At Agra, Nersingh Deo presented the Emperor with a white leopard, of which colour no one had ever before been seen. The ground of the skin was a dirty white and the spots were grey.[2] Jehangir, in his memoirs, observes, that he had seen an antelope, a hawk, a sparrow, a crow, a patridge, a quail, and a peacock, that were white, but had never before even heard of a white leopard.*

About this time, Jehangir married the daugnter of Kaim Khan Arab, one of the principal nobles of the late Emperor, and who had taught Jehangir the use of the bow. This Begum shortly after obtained the title of Padshah Mahl, or monarch of the seraglio.

Intelligence being received from Bengal, of the death of Jehangir Kuly Khan the Subahdar, Islam Khan was appointed to succeed him, and Sheikh Afzul Khan, son of Sheikh Abulfazel, succeeded Islam Khan in the government of Bahar.[3]

The Ranna having again revolted, Mehabut Khan marched against him with twelve thousand

[1] R. B. I. 137-8.

[2] R. B. I. 140. 'Its spots were of blue colour and the whiteness of the body was also inclined to bluishness.'

* Governor Hastings sent from Bengal a black leopard which was presented to His Majesty, the King of England, and is now in the Tower of London: the spots are of a deeper black than the prevailing colour of the skin.

[3] R. B. I. 142-3.

cavalry, two thousand Berkundaze infantry, sixty elephants, eighty pieces of cannon and gujnals* and a supply of twenty lakhs of rupees.[1]

The Khankhanan, upon his return from Burhanpoor, presented peishkush of rubies, emeralds, and pearls with ninety elephants, altogether estimated at three lakhs of rupees, besides other articles of considerable value.

About this time Kishen Singh[2] gained a victory over the Ranna, of whose army twenty persons of distinction were killed and near three thousand men taken prisoners.[3]

Jehangir, attended by all the nobility, went on foot to the shrine of Akber, where he bestowed in charity a considerable sum of money. He gave orders for the mausoleum to be re-built, upon a magnificent plan; and fifteen lakhs of rupees were expended on these improvements.[4]

At the death of Akber, affairs in the Dekhan fell into great confusion; many of the chiefs threw off the yoke, and the imperial army not being able to resist them any longer, the Khankhanan entered into a written engagement with the Emperor, to make a complete conquest of the Dekhan in the course of two years, provided he was allowed a reinforcement of twelve thousand cavalry, and a supply of ten lakhs of rupees. These demands being immediately complied with, he began his

* A gujnal is a small gun fixed on the back of an elephant.

[1] R. B. I. 145; Iqbal, p. 34; Khaf. I. 259.

[2] An Officer under Mahabat Khan.

[3] R. B. I. 151; Tod. I. 282.

[4] R. B. I. 152. Owing to the revolt of Khusru Jahangir had had to start for Lahore and the architects had built it after their own design.

march to the Dekhan, on the 14th of Shaban, or 4th December, accompanied by Rajah Soorej Singh.[1]

Repeated complaints having been made to his Majesty, that the relations and dependants of Mortiza Khan had variously oppressed the inhabitants of Ahmedabad, he was ordered to court. Azem Khan was appointed Subahdar of Gujerat, but to remain with the Emperor and depute to that government Jehangir Kuly Khan, his eldest son. Mortiza Khan, on his return to court, was pardoned; and shortly after obtained a considerable jageer.[2]

Mirza Berkhoordar, son of Mirza Abdulrahman, obtained the title of Khan Alum.[3] His great grandfather entered into the service of Timour and his descendants were successively Omrahs of high rank.

Mehabat Khan[4] not having made any progress in the war against the Ranna, the command of the army, in that quarter, was now conferred upon Abdullah Khan.[5]

Sultan Jehandar, one of the illegitimate sons of the Emperor, who had gone into Bengal with Kotebeddeen Koka,* having shwon some symptoms of insanity,[6] was now sent to court. At the same time Sultan Shiriar, his twin brother, came also to Agra from Gujerat.

1 Khaf. I 259; R. B. I., 149, 153; M. J. p. 60.
2 R. B. I., 153.
3 R. B. I., 154.
4 R. B. I., 155-6.
5 For his life see Maasir I, 97-105.
6 Mazub-i-madar-zad probably meaning a born idiot R. B. I., 15-6.

The Khankhanan proving dilatory in his operations, Sultan Purveiz was sent into the Dekhan[1] with twenty lakhs of rupees, accompanied by Jaffer Beg Asof Khan, in the capacity of Ataleek.[2] The prince's jageer of Khandies and Berar was increased by the addition of the fort of Asseergarh. A short time after, a reinforcement of seven thousand cavalry, which Khanjehan Khan,[3] and other officers of rank and high renown, were sent from Agra, and Rajah Nersingh Deo, Shujahut Khan, and Rajah Birkirmajeet were ordered to join them at Oujein with five thousand more cavalry.

Abdullah Khan, soon after he obtained the command, gained a considerable victory over the Ranna,[4] and blockaded him in the narrow passes of the mountains; for which service[5] he was promoted to the rank of five thousand cavalry, with the title of Firoze Jung Bahadre.

A calender presented to his Majesty a full-grown tiger, which, having been trained from a cub, was perfectly tame. He was let loose in the plain of the Jerokha at Agra, near the river; and afterwards fourteen or fifteen others were tamed in like manner, and allowed to range at large in the same place.

The Emperor now married the daughter of Rajah Ramchund Bundeyleh.[6]

[1] Where his Court at Burhanpur is described by Roe, pp. 70, 79.
[2] R. B. I., 156-7; M. J. p. 61; Iqbal, 36-7; Khaf. I. 260.
[3] R. B. I., 161; Iqbal, 38-9.
[4] R. B. I. 251 over Karan the heir-apparent of the Rana.
[5] According to the Tuzuk (R. B. 155) the promotion was on his appointment to the command.

About this time, he went on a hunting party to the Pergunnah of Bary. On these excursions, he was so careful that the ryots should not suffer any injury, that he appointed proper officers to protect the crops, and to ascertain the actual damage sustained; which was always made good to the sufferers.[1]

He now pardoned Abdulrahman who had been so active in Khusru's rebellion and survived the severe punishment already described.[2]

Upon the Emperor's return to Agra, Mocurreb Khan, who was just arrived there from Surat, presented him with some curious Europe plate, and other valuable articles. At the same time, the Khankhanan sent him the Yousef Zelikha of Jami, copied by Moulla Meer Ali, beautifully illuminated and valued at a thousand gold mohurs.[3]

A poor widow of Cambayit complained to Jehangir that Mocurreb Khan, the Governor of that place had forcibly taken away her daughter, and that when she demanded the girl from him, he pretended she was dead. The Emperor ordered the matter to be investigated, and it being proved upon the person who had been the agent in the business, he was severely punished;[4] and half of Mocurreb Khan's jageer was taken from him, and transferred to the widow, for her maintenance.[5]

The perhunnah of Curreckpoor having been conferred in jageer upon Afzul Khan, the Subahdar

[1] R. B. I. 163.
[2] R. B. I. 164.
[3] R. B. I. 167-8.
[4] Jahangir (R. B. I. 172) says the man was put to death.
[5] Also he 'reduced Muqarrab Khan's mansab by one half and made an allowance to the woman who had been thus injured '.

of Bahar, he set out to visit his new grant, and left the city of Patna under the charge of Sheikh Hassam Bannarassy, and Ghiass Zein Khan, with only a small number of troops, as the country was then in a state of perfect tranquility. But one Koteb, a man of low extraction, thinking it a favourable time for exciting an insurrection, pretended that he was Sultan Khusru, escaped from the prison, and with an artful tale and large promises he deceived some and bribed many others to join him.

A. H. 1019—A. D. 1610.

When he saw his party sufficiently strong, he suddenly entered the fort of Patna, and Sheikh Bannarassy, and Ghiasszein Khan, being totally unprepared for resistance, made their escape out of a window,[1] and getting into a boat, fled to Currukpoor, which is about 60 cose distant. The rebels found in the fort treasure to a considerable amount; and their number increased daily. The first intelligence brought to Afzul Khan was that the prince had actually made his appearance; but he was soon undeceived by authentic accounts, and shortly after the fugitives joined him at Currukpoor. Afzul Khan made all possible haste to Patna. The impostor drew out his men on the banks of the river Punpun, where a battle was fought, in which Koteb and his party, after a faint resistance, were totally routed. They fled to the city of Patna but were so closely pursued by the victors, as not to have time to shut the gates after

[1] R. B. I. 174 'by a wicket gate'.

them. The impostor, and a few of his adherents, possessed themselves of the house of Afzul Khan, which they barricaded and defended resolutely for some hours killing about thirty of the assailants with arrows; but at length all his party being destroyed, he delivered himself up to Afzul Khan, who, in revenge for the dishonour which he had done to his house, put him to death immediately[1] and all those who had before been taken prisoners, were ordered into close confinement. The Emperor, enraged at the negligence and pusillanimity of Sheikh Bannarassy and Ghiasszein Khan, had them brought to court. Their beards were shaved, after which they were dressed in women's clothes, placed upon asses, and led about the city of Agra.[2]

The Khankhanan neglecting to lay in proper supplies for the support of his numerous army, and having led them to Balaghaut, found himself exposed to famine: to avoid which, he concluded a dishonourable peace, and marched to Burhanpoor, after having lost the important fortress of Ahmednagar, which had been conquered in the time of Akber. The whole army being dissatisfied with his conduct, a general complaint was sent against him to the Emperor, in consequence whereof he was re-called, and the command of the army conferred upon Khanjehan Khan.[3] The Emperor soon after sent a reinforcement, along with Khan Azem, with thirty lakhs of rupees for the payment of the

[1] 'On the same day' according to R. B. I. 175.
[2] R. B. I., M. 3-76; Iqbal, 42-4; M. J. 65; Khaf. I. 261.
[3] R. B. I. 178-80; Iqbal, 38-9; Khaf. I. 261-2.

troops, and four lakhs of rupees to defray his own expenses.[1] The Khankhanan on his arrival at court, met with a very cool reception; but a short time after, his son Irej obtained the title of Shanowaz Khan.[2]

A. H. 1020—A. D. 1611.

In the beginning of this year, arrived at Agra, Yeadgar Aly Sultan, ambassador from Shah Abbas, king of Persia. He brought from his Majesty, a letter containing warm professions of friendship, and several Iraky horses, with other valuable presents. Upon delivering the letter, a present of thirty thousand rupees was ordered him from the treasury.[3]

About this time were celebrated the nuptials of Sultan Khorum, with the daughter of Mozuffer Hussain Mirza Seffevee.[4]

A dangerous insurrection now broke out at Cabul, headed by Ahdad an Afghan, who, with his party, attempted to take that city by surprise; but were repulsed by the garrison, and the inhabitants, with great slaughter.[5] The Emperor thinking that Khandowran, and the other officers stationed at Lahoor, were remiss in their efforts against the Afghans, ordered upon this service, Keleetch Khan, and appointed him Subahdar of Cabul. The Subahdary of Penjab was conferred upon Mortiza Khan; but he was permitted to conduct the

[1] R. B. I. 183-84.
[2] R. B. I, 197.
[3] R. B. I. 193-6.
[4] R. B. I. 180.
[5] R. B. I., 197-8, 263, 311-312; Price, 164-5.

business through agents and continue himself at Court.

The Khankhanan, soon after being re-called from the Dekhan, obtained in jageer the sircars of Culpee and Kenoje, in Agra [1]; and was sent to preserve peace in that quarter.

The most remarkable event of this reign is the marriage[2] of the Emperor with Mehr-ul-Nessa, Begum, the daughter of Etemadeddowlah, and widow of Sheer Afkun.[3] Upon the death of her husband, the relations of the late Kotebeddeen sent her to court; and the Emperor, in his affliction for the loss of his friend, committed her to the charge of Rokiah Sultana, Begum, one of Akber's widows, with whom she lived, unnoticed by the Emperor, till the present festival of the new year,[4] when seeing her by accident, he was so captivated by her extraordinary beauty, that he married her immediately.[5] He then gave her the title of Nour Mahl*, and some years after,[6] that of Nourjehan† Begum‡. Her father, Etemadeddowlah,[7] was raised to the Vekalut; and Abulhassan, her eldest brother, obtained the title of Etekad Khan,[8] with the office of Khansaman.§ Her power over the Emperor soon became absolute, and all affairs of the state

1 R. B. I., 199.
2 Not mentioned in the Tuzuk.
3 Iqbal, 55 E. D. VI, 404; Khaf. I, 265-6; Maasir, I, 130; III, 622-5.
4 Hadi E. D. 397-8.
5 Four years and a few days after the death of Sher Afkun, Price. p. 46-7.
* The light of the Seraglio.
6 *i.e.*, in the 11th year *i.e.*, in 1616, R. B. I. 319; Iqbal, 56; Della Valle, I, 53-4. Peter Mundy II, 205-6.
† The Light of the World.
‡ Princess.
7 R. B. I. 22,200.
8 R. B. I. 202.
§ Steward of the household.

were committed to her management.[1] She sat behind a Chegh * at the window of the Jarokha, whilst many of the nobility paid her the compliment of the Khoornish and Tesleem. Her name was inscribed upon the coin, and excepting that she was not prayed for in the Khotbah, she was, in every respect, the absolute monarch of the empire. The following is the inscription upon her coin:

"AT THE COMMAND OF THE EMPEROR, JEHANGIR, THE COIN HAS OBTAINED AN HUNDRED ORNAMENTS; FROM THE NAME OF NOURJEHAN PADSHAH BEGUM".

Abdullah Khan pursued his victory over the Ranna, who fled into the mountains. Abdullah Khan was rewarded with the Subahdary of Gujerat; where he was ordered to raise forces, and proceed to the Dekhan for which purpose he received a supply of four lakhs of rupees. Rajah Bassoo was sent to pursue the military operations against the Ranna.[2]

The Emperor went on a hunting party to Summergurh, near Agra. The nets were spread according to custom, and the pavilions of the Harem pitched within the enclosure. In the course of a week nine hundred and seventy deer were taken. Two hundred and forty-one were ordered to be sent to Futtehpoor, and let loose upon the plains of Chowgong; and about a hundred had

[1] Roe, 325.

* A skreen or fine lattice, through which a person may look without being discovered.

[2] R. B. I. 200.

silver rings put in their noses, after which they were set at liberty. The rest that were killed or wounded, were distributed amongst the Omrahs and Munsebdars.

A. H. 1021—A. D. 1612.

The method of making atyr of roses, was now first discovered by the mother of Nourjehan Begum. The atyr is the essential oil of roses, a very small proportion of which floats upon the surface of distilled rose water, whilst it is warm, and is collected by means of a piece of cotton fastened upon a stick. It is the most delicate perfume that is known, being as exquisite as the scent of a new blown rose. The Emperor presented the inventress with a string of valuable pearls ; and Selima Sultana Begum, one of Akber's widows, named this essence ATVR JEHANGIRY or THE ESSENCE OF JEHANGIR.[1]

One of the most remarkable events of this year, was the defeat of the Afghans, in Bengal, and the death of their leader Osman.[2] Bengal measures from Chittagong to Ghurry, four hundred and fifty cose in longitude, and from the northern mountains to sircar Maduran, is two hundred cose in latitude. The revenue at this time was estimated at sixty crore of dams or sicca rupees 1,50,00,000. The military establishment, in the time of Akber, consisted of twenty thousand cavalry, one hundred

[1] R. B. I. 270-D.
[2] R. B. I. 207-15.

thousand infantry, two thousand elephants,[1] four or five thousand armed boats and a train of artillery. At the death of Shere Khan, his son Sileem Khan, possessed himself of all Bengal; and was succeeded therein by Soliman Gernnee. Akber's army drove out the Afghans from the interior parts: but some of them settled on the boundaries, especially about the Dacca districts, where they fortified themselves. At the head of these was Osman Afghan, who gained several advantages over the forces of Akber, and particularly during the government of Rajah Mansingh, who, despairing of subduing him, at length suffered him to remain unmolsted. But, Islam Khan, the present Subahdar, sent Shujahut Khan with a large army against him. An obstinate battle was fought in which Shujahut Khan was thrown from his elephant, but recovered himself; Osman was slain and all his adherents submitted to the conqueror. The Emperor rewarded Shujahut Khan by an increase of munseb, with the additional title of Rustam Zemanee. Islam Khan removed the seat of his Government to Dacca, and gave to his new city the name of Jehangirabad, or the City of Jehangir.

About this time, Mocurreb Khan was sent to conclude a treaty with the Portuguese Viceroy at Goa. After transacting that business, he returned with all the curiosities he could procure; and which he bought at whatever price the Portuguese thought proper to demand. Jehangir mentions, in

[1] 1,000 according to the Tuzuk, R. B. I. 207.

his Toozek, that Mocurreb Khan brought from Goa several curious birds and beasts, and, amongst them, describes a turkey cock, as a bird that he had never before seen.[1]

The Emperor, tired with the lingering operations in the Dekhan, formed a plan for terminating the war at one blow.[2] Abdullah Khan was ordered to march his army from Gujerat, through the passes of Nassick Terbunek, whilst Khanjehan Khan proceeded by the way of Berar. Had they properly concerted their measures, their united forces must infallibly have reduced the enemy to such straights, as would have compelled them to conclude a peace on the most advantageous terms for the Emperor. But, unfortunately, the two generals envied and hated each other, and sooner than act in concert, suffered the whole plan to prove abortive. Abdullah Khan, flattering himself that his army alone was sufficiently strong for ensuring the conquest, was unwilling to allow Khanjehan Khan any share in the glory that would have attended the conclusion of the war. He, therefore, marched hastily from Gujerat, without giving the other any advice of his motions, and entered the passes Nassick Terbunek, where the Bargees harassed him with skirmishes by day, and at night infested the camp with rockets and other fireworks, in the discharge of which they possessed singular skill. Khanjehan Khan and Rajah Mansingh, received intelligence of the situation, but

[1] R. B. I. 215.
[2] R. B. I. 155.

were so dilatory in marching to his relief, that he was obliged to lead back his army to Ahmedabad, by the way of Dowletabad, whilst the enemy hung upon his rear, and infested his march to the very borders of Baglana. When Khanjehan Khan and Rajah Mansingh heard of his retreat, having thereby gained their ends, they marched back to Adilabad, and joined the army under the command of Sultan Purveiz.[1] Upon this ill success his Majesty was persuaded to send the Khankhanan again into the Dekhan, hoping at last to derive benefit from his experience. He was accordingly recalled from Kinoje and ordered to the Dekhan, along with his sons Shahnowaz Khan and Darab Khan.[2]

Soon after the above mentioned ill success in the Dekhan, Asof Khan died of a chronic disorder, at Burhanpoor, in the sixtieth year of his age. Besides the advantages of a graceful and beautiful person, he was endowed with profound judgment, uncommon eloquence, and ready wit, was an elegant prose writer, and possessed considerable poetical talents.[3] Also, about the same time, died, in his Government at Kandahar, Mirza Ghazi, a gallant soldier, and a faithful subject; but unfortunately addicted to drinking to which vice he fell a victim.[4]

Sultan Khorum now married the daughter of Etekad Khan, the eldest brother of Nourjehan

[1] R. B. I. 219-21; Iqbal, 65-6; Khaf. I. 273-6.
[2] R. B. I. 221.
[3] R. B. I. 222-3.
[4] R. B. I. 223.

Begum. The nuptials were celebrated with uncommon magnificence and splendour, at the palace of Etemadeddowlah, the bride's grandfather; and his Majesty honoured the ceremony with his presence.[1]

Shujahut Khan had been ordered to Orissa by Islam Khan, and as he was travelling on an elephant, at night, happened to pass by another of these animals picketted near the road, and who being frightened at the sound of the horses feet, attempted to break his chains. The attendants called out to apprize Shujahut Khan of his danger, who, waking suddenly, threw himself on the ground, and happening to alight upon his hands amongst some rubbish, broke some of his fingers, and being of a bad habit of body, this accident occasioned his death a few days after.[2]

Motaked Khan, late Dewan of Bengal, now arrived at court, and Islam Khan took that opportunity of sending to the Emperor, the sons and other relations of the deceased Osman Khan Afghan. They presented their peishkush which was graciously received.[3] Motaked Khan was at this time appointed Meer Bukhshee; and Zuffer Khan obtained the Subahdary of Bahar.

After much felicitation, Khan Azem was appointed to command the army employed against the Ranna; and now set out for Malwah, where

[1] R. B. I. 224 and *note*.

[2] R. B. I. 226-7.

[3] R. B. I. 230.

his jageer was situated, to make the necessary preparations for prosecuting the war.[1]

A. H. 1022—A. D. 1613.

Housheng, son of Islam Khan, arrived at court, and brought with him some of the people called Mughs, who had lately been taken prisoners. They inhabit the islands of Bengal, and are mere brutes in human form. They eat all kinds of animals, nothing being to them unclean. They marry their sisters[2], that are by another mother. Their features bear a great resemblance to the Calmuc Tartars; but their language has no mixture of Turkish, being very familiar to that used in Tibet. They profess no religion, nor have any faith in their dealings.

Afzul Khan, son of the great Abulfazel, who had come from his government of Bahar to pay his respects to the Emperor, died at Agra of boils which had turned into incurable ulcers.[3]

The hall of public audience is separated by two balustrades:—within the first rail, none but persons of high rank are admitted; all other servents of the crown are allowed to pass the second rail; and the multitude stand without side. Formerly both rails were of wood; but now the inner one was ordered to be made of silver as well as the stairs to ascend from thence to the Jerokha; and two wooden elephants, one on each side of the Jerokha, were taken down, and in their stead were

[1] R. B. I. 234 Price 220-2.

[2] R. B. I. 236.

[3] R. B. I. 241.

placed two of silver, weighing one hundred and twenty-five maunds, in value about four lakhs of rupees.[1]

A hot pestilential blast of wind at Bahmenabad (Amanabad) twelve cose from Lahoor, killed nine men who were standing under a tree; the birds fell lifeless from its branches; and many beasts were found dead in the neighbouring fields.[2]

The Emperor now undertook a journey to Ajmeer,[3] for the purpose of visiting the shrine of Khojeh Moyeneddeen Chiesty, as well as to have a nearer control over the operations in the Dekhan, and against the Ranna. When he came in sight of the shrine, at the distance of about ten miles, he alighted from his horse, and walked to the tomb, where he performed his devotions, and distributed large sums in charity.[4]

He at this time received intelligence, that the Portuguese at Goa, regardless of the treaty lately concluded, had seized some merchantships near the port of Surat, and made several Musalmans prisoners. Mocurreb Khan, in whose Government Surat was situated, was ordered to make a particular investigation of their conduct.[5]

The Emperor now sent Sultan Khorum to command against the Ranna, and although this procedure was at the particular request of Khan Azem, yet when it came to the point, he was

[1] R. B. I. 242.

[2] R. B. I. 247-48.

[3] Said to have been suggested by Khan Azam.

[4] R. B. I. 253-54.

[5] R. B. I. 255.

jealous of the Prince's authority, and behaved with such disrespect, that he was ordered to court and from thence sent prisoner to Gualiar. Shortly after, he was restored to liberty, in consequence of Jehangir seeing in a dream the late Emperor, who intreated for his pardon. He then obtained a Tunkha equivalent to the maintenance of five thousand cavalry, and his son Jehangir Kuly Khan, with his other relations, were permitted to go to Allahabad, where their jageer was situated.[1]

Islam Khan having died suddenly in Bengal, his brother, Gossim Khan was appointed his successor in that Government.[2]

Whilst the Emperor was at Ajmeer, a brass kettle was made, measuring ten yards in height, and ten yards in diameter, and in it was dressed victuals for five thousand persons, which was distributed at the tomb of Moyeneddeen Chiesty.

At the intercession of his mother and sisters, Sultan Khusru was now set at liberty, and permitted to come to court as formerly. But as he did not seem satisfied, or even sensible of the indulgence, he was shortly after again banished from his father's presence.[3]

A. H. 1023—A. D. 1613.

Etekad Khan, son of Etemadeddowlah, now obtained the title of Asof Khan;[4] and Ibrahim Khan, the maternal uncle of the Empress Nour

[1] R. B. I. 257-8. 261, 269, 287, 289.

[2] R. B. I. 257.

[3] R. B. I. 252, 261.

[4] R. B. I. 260, 278.

Mahal, was appointed second Bukhshee of the household.

A princess was born to Sultan Khorum, by the daughter of Asof Khan, whom the Emperor named Jehan Ara Begum.

About this time Ahdad and his rebellious Afghans were defeated at Kabul by Mohamed Khan, who made a pyramid of five hundred[1] of their heads. He was rewarded with the title of Lushker Khan.[2]

Rajah Mansingh now died in the Dekhan; upon which his son Behow Singh was ordered to court, and on his arrival, the Emperor confirmed him in all his late father's possessions, with the title of Mirza Rajah.[3]

At the pass of Hasez Jemal, in the neighbourhood of Ajmeer, is a delightful spring of water, near to which Jehangir ordered a magnificent palace to be erected. A stone basin forty yards square, was made to receive the water, of this spring through artificial fountains that spouted to the height of twelve yards. To this place he gave the name of Cheshmeh Nour, or the fountain of light.[4]

When Sultan Khorum arrived at Oudypoor, the Ranna's capital, he detached bodies of troops into all parts of the country, and so completely hemmed him up in the mountains, that all supplies

[1] 600 heads according to the Tuzuk R. B. I. 264.

[2] R. B. I. 263-4. According to price (p. 94) the prisoners were brough before Jahangir with the decapitated heads of 17,000 suspended from their necks.

[3] R. B. I. 266. The clan of Mahasingh, son of Jagat Singh. Man Singh his eldest son who had predeceased his father was thus overlooked.

[4] R. B. I. 269-70.

were cut off; a malignant disorder raged amongst the troops from a stagnated air, and desertions became very frequent. Thus reduced to extremities, the Ranna deputed to the Prince, Soob Kurren and Hirdoss Jehlah, two of his principal servants, to intreat that confidential persons might be sent to assure him of honourable terms, upon his making due submission to the Emperor. The prince sent to him Mirza Shukerullah, his Dewan, and Soonder Doss, his Meer Saman, to promise a favourable reception. When he returned with them and approached the camp, the Prince did him further honour, by sending Abdullah Khan, Rajah Soorej Mull, Rajah Nersingh Deo, and other officers of rank to meet him.

A few days after, the Prince gave a grand entertainment at Gowkundeh, when Ranna Amer Singh was ordered to be introduced. At his entrance, from the place whence he first discovered the Prince seated on a throne, at every step as he advanced he made the Tesleem: and when he reached the throne, prostrated himself with his forehead upon the ground. The Prince, laying hold of both his hands, lifted him up and embraced him. When these ceremonies were ended Abdullah Khan, and Soorej Singh, were ordered to seat themselves on the right, and the Ranna on the left side of the throne. The Prince entered into familiar conversation with the Ranna, and filled him with joy and confidence. He presented the Prince with a ruby a valuable family jewel. The Rana was honoured with a magnificent khelut, a sword and

Khenjer inlaid with precious stones, a horse and an elephant, both richly caparisoned; and all his suite received dresses suitable to their respective ranks. When the Ranna took his leave, Mirza Shukerullah Khan, and Soonder Doss, were ordered to escort to court his son Kurren, and they returned with him in the afternoon. He met with a most gracious reception, and received khelut and other presents; and it being agreed that he should accompany the Prince to the Emperor, fifty thousand rupees were issued from the treasury to defray the expenses of his journey.[1]

Sultan Khorum gained great renown by this victory, the Ranna of Oudypoor having never before been subdued by the Kings of Delhi nor by any Emperor of the house of Timour. Akber had an army constantly employed against him, but was never able to gain any considerable advantage.

A. H. 1014—A. D. 1615.

As soon as Sultan Khorum had settled affairs with the Ranna[2] he set out for, Ajmeer with Ranna's son Kurren.[3] When Sultan Khorum encamped within sight of Ajmeer, he was met by the prime minister and all the principal nobility. The royal palace was decorated in the most magnificent manner for his reception, and a grand entertainment prepared on the occasion.

In the morning, Sultan Khorum entered the city of Ajmeer on horse-back, attended by all the

[1] R. B. I. 273-6 Iebal, 77 Khaf. 279.

[2] The Rana feeling himself humiliated by the defeat and disgrace of surrender abdicated in favour of Kara—Tod I. 291-2.

[3] R. B. I. 276. Khaf I, 279.

great officers of State, and the Munsebdars with their troops.[1] About two o'clock he waited upon the Emperor. After the Prince had paid the usual compliments of the Koornish, Tesleem and Zemeenbose, his Majesty arose from the throne, and folded him in his arms, with every demonstration of paternal joy and affection. His nuzzer was a thousand mohurs, and a thousand rupees, and a thousand mohurs in Tesedduk*, together with a crystal basket[2] full of Jewels, and the ruby which had been given him by the Ranna, valued at fifty thousand rupees.[3] He received a khelut, richly ornamented with pearls, a horse and an elephant richly caparisoned: and the Dewan Azem was ordered to prepare for him tunkhas equivalent to twenty thousand zat and ten thousand cavalry. Kurren[4] then made his submissions, after which he was permitted to stand on the left side of the Jarokha. Kurren was honoured with a rich dress, and all the Omrahs who had served under the Prince were distinguished with marks of the royal favour, according to their merits. All the lands conquered from the Ranna, during the last sixty years, all of which had been granted in jageer, were restored to him, upon his becoming tributary to the Emperor.

About this time the Portuguese Viceroy attempted to seize the castle of Surat but was

[1] R. B. I. 277-8.

* Or to be distributed in charity.

[2] 'Of Frank work' R. B. I. 286.

[3] Sixty thousand rupees according to the Tuzak, R. B. I. 285.

[4] Roe 127.

repulsed by the English, who resided there under the Emperor's protection. The English, with their fireworks, burnt several of the ships belonging to the Portuguese, and gave them so warm a reception, that finding themselves unequal to the enterprise, they were glad to retreat. They then sent a person to Mocurreb Khan, the Governor of Surat, pretending that having gone to conclude treaty, the English commenced this unprovoked hostility. This account is taken from Jehangir's Memoirs.[1]

At the recommendation of Sultan Khorum, Mirza Shukerullah obtained the title of Afzul Khan, and Soonder Doss that of Rajah Bickermajeet.[2]

Dyanet Khan,[3] without any provocation, having behaved with great insolence to Etemadeddowlah, his Majesty was so enraged thereat, that he ordered him to be sent prisoner to Gualiar; but a few months after, at the intercession of Etemadeddowlah, he was released from his confinement.[4]

From the commencement of his reign, the Emperor had ordered that on every Friday night, all necessitous persons should be brought to him; and he relieved their wants with money, grants of land etc. From the accounts kept by the officers of Government it appeared, he had this year bestowed as follows: in money fifty thousand rupees; of land fourteen whole villages, and one lakh ninety

[1] R. B. I. 274-5.
[2] R. B. I. 402.
[3] Sabit Khan according to R. B. I. 278.
[4] R. B. I. 278-9, 303, 306, 318.

thousand beegahs; twenty-six ploughs, and eleven thousand kherwars* of rice.[1]

During the celebration of the festival of the new year, the munseb of Etemadeddowlah was increased to six thousand zat, and three thousand cavalry, with the privilege to beat the nekareh** at the residence of the court; an honour which no one, excepting the king's sons, enjoyed.[2] At the same time Kurren was appointed a Munsebdar of five thousand zat and five thousand cavalry.[3] He was the first of his family who had ever entered into the service, or acknowledged obedience to any foreign power.

On the 29th of Seffer, or 19th March, Sultan Dara Shekuuh, was born to Sultan Khorum by the daughter of Asof Khan.[4]

Mustefa Beg, ambassador from Shah Abbass, arrived at Ajmeer, to announce to the Emperor his conquest of Gurjestan or Georgia. He brought many valuable presents, amongst which were horses, mules, Aleppo cloths, and nine Europe dogs trained for hunting.[5]

Mehabut Khan made his Majesty very considerable presents, amongst which was a kepauh* inlaid with precious stones valued at a lakh of

* The kherwar is about three maunds.

1 R. B. I. 279.

** A drum, beaten only by persons of high rank.

2 R. B. I. 280-1.

3 R. B. I. 281.

4 R. B. I. 282.

5 R. B. I. 282-3.

* A long sword.

rupees; and other articles which were moreover estimated at one lakh thirty-eight thousand rupees.[1]

Ibrahim Khan was now appointed Soobahdar of Bahar, in the room of Zuffer Khan, recalled.

In the beginning of this year, Kurren obtained permission to return to his father. During his residence at court, he received from the Emperor in money and jewels, to the amount of ten[2] lakhs of rupees, with one hundred and ten horses and five elephants. And the present which were conferred upon him by Sultan Khorum were also of great value**. A short time after the departure of Kurren, his son, Jugget Singh arrived at court, and was graciously received.

When Sultan Khorum entered the twenty-fourth year of his age, the Emperor made a grand entertainment on the occasion. The Prince having never yet tasted wine, Jehangir filled a glass, which he put into his hand, and told him he ought to follow the example of his ancestors by drinking the juice of the grape; but however advised him to use it with moderation, quoting the following lines from Abu Aly Sina*.

> "Wine is the enemy of the ignorant, and the friend of the wise:
> A small quantity is teriac**, when drunk to excess, it is a poisonous snake:

[1] R. B. I. 284.

[2] Two lakhs according to the Tuzuk; R. B. I. 293.

** This account, which is taken from Jehangir's Memoirs, is probably exaggerated.

* Vulgarly called, by European authors, Avicenna.

** An antidote.

An intemperate use thereof is destructive;
But taken in moderation, it proves beneficial to the constitution".[1]

Near the end of this year, Shanowaz Khan, son of the Khankhanan gained some advantage over Amber, the general, and prime-minister of Nizam-ul-mulk.

The most remarkable event of this year, was the conquest of Gookerah*** dependant upon Bahar. Diamonds are obtained from one of its rivers after the following manner: During the dry season, the river discovers great part of its bed, in which are small cavities, where the water still remains; and such of them as harbour swarms of gnats, contain diamonds. The people throw out the water, and by digging down about a yard and a half, find amongst the gravel and sand, diamonds of different sizes, some single stones worth a lakh of rupees, and others very small. This bed of the river which produces diamonds, is in the zemindary of Dirjen Sal. No former Soobahdar of Bahar had ever been able to penetrate into his country, on account of the thickness of the jungles, and the unhealthiness of the air; and, therefore, after making some fruitless attempts, were contented to allow him to remain in peace, in return for a tribute of a few valuable stones. But Ibrahim Khan, the new Soobahdar, suddenly marched into his country with a large force, and before the Rajah could assemble his troops, took

[1] R. B. I. 306.

*** It is now generally written Goorkah.

him prisoner, and annexed his zemindary to the empire. For this eminent service his munseb was raised to four thousand zat and five thousand cavalry, which the title of Futteb Jung* and all his officers were largely rewarded.[1]

The festival of the new year was celebrated at Ajmeer with great magnificence. Mehr-ul-Nissa, who on her marriage with the Emperor was styled Nour Mahl**, now obtained the title of Nurjehan*** Begum.[2] Amongst the presents made to the Emperor, during the festival was a khenjer, valued at fifty thousand rupees, from Meer Jemaleddeen Hussein Anjew.

During these holidays, the Emperor honoured Asof Khan with a visit, on which occasion, the road was covered with velvet and brocades that cost ten thousand rupees.

He also went to the house of Etemadeddowlah, who presented a nuzzer of great value, out of which his Majesty accepted of jewels to the amount of a lakh and twenty thousand rupees. The munseb of this nobleman was now increased to seven thousand zat, and five thousand cavalry with a Teman Towgh* and permission to beat his nekareh, immediately after that of Sultan Khorum.

About this time died Morteza Khan, whilst he was besieging the fort of Kengerah, whither he had been sent a few months before.[3]

* The victorious in war.
[1] R. B. I. 315.
** The light of the seraglio.
*** The light of the world.
[2] Roe, 125-6, 131, 132; R. B. I. 319.
* *Vide* Ayeen Akbery, Vol. I, page 65.
[3] R. B. I. 324.

A son was now born to Sultan Khorum, by the daughter of Asof Khan and the Emperor named him Shah Shujah.[1]

At Ajmeer the Emperor was weighed with the usual ceremonies, on the solar and lunar anniversaries of his nativity.[2]

About this time arrived at Ajmeer Mohammed Reza Beg, ambassador from Shah Abbass.

A. H. 1025—A. D. 1616.

Abed Khan Bukhshee and the Vakil Navees, having represented from Ahmedabad, that Abdullah Khan the Soobahdar, displeased with them for writing to Court all the transactions of his Government, had enraged a number of people to attack and insult them on their way home; the Emperor was so enraged thereat, that he ordered Dyanet Khan to go and bring him prisoner to Court. But Abdullah Khan having received secret intelligence of the Emperor's intentions, set out from Ahmedabad on foot, and meeting with Dyanet Khan in the middle of the way, was with difficulty prevailed upon to make use of a palkee, during the remainder of the road to Court.[3] When he arrived at Ajmeer, Sultan Khorum interceded with the Emperor, and obtained his pardon.*

[1] R. B. I. 328.

[2] Roe, 221-2.

[3] R. B. I. 331; For interesting details of the affair, see Roe, 242.

* Sir Thomas Roe, the ambassador from James the First of England to Jehangir was then at Ajmeer, and in his journal are mentioned most of the events of this year, which we have related from the Masr Jehangiry. The reader will find great amusement in reading Sir Thomas Roe's journal published in Churchill's Collection of Voyages and Travels, Vol. I.

By the command of the Emperor, the shrine of Moyeneddeen Chiesty was surrounded with a gold railing of pierced work, which cost one lakh and twelve thousand rupees.[1]

Mocurreb Khan presented the Emperor with a young Ethiopian Elephant. His ears were larger than those of Hindostan, the proboscis and tail somewhat longer. Some years before this, Etemad Khan sent Akber a young Ethiopian Elephant, which, when it was full grown, was active but very vicious.[2]

The plague first appeared in Punjab, and from thence spread to Lahore ; and after it had somewhat abated in that quarter, broke out in the Duab and Delhi, where it committed great devastation. This disorder had never before been known in Hindostan. The physicians attributed it to there having been a great drought for two years together, which they supposed had infected the air.[3]

Whilst the Emperor was at Ajmeer, he received from the Dekhan marble statues of Ranna Amer Singh, and his son Kurren which were allowed to bear strong resemblance of the originals. They were ordered to be carried to Agra, and placed in the garden of the Jarokha Dursun.[4]

Khusru was now taken out of the charge of Annyroy Singhdelum and committed to the custody of Asof Khan.[5]

[1] According to R. B. I. 329, 1,10,000 rupees.

[2] R. B. I. 323.

[3] R. B. I. 330, Iqbal, 88-9.

[4] 'For certain considerations' R. B. I. 336 ; Roe, 245, 246, 256.

[5] R. B. I. 332.

Muhammad Reza Beg, ambassador from Shah Abbas, waited upon the Emperor at Ajmeer, and presented to him a complimentary letter with some valuable presents from the King of Persia.[1]

Through the mismanagement of Sultan Purveiz affairs in the Dekhan were declining daily; the enemy having by degrees driven him out of all the country from Ballaghaut to Ahmednagar. Sultan Khorum's great success against the Ranna, determined the Emperor[2] to give him the command in the Dekhan, whilst he himself advanced as far as Mendow. On this occasion, he bestowed upon Khorum the title of Shah, or King, a dignity hitherto confined to the Emperors of the house of Timour.[3] His munseb was increased to twenty thousand zat and ten thousand cavalry, of two and three horses*. At the time that these honours were conferred, he received a splendid khelut, embroidered with pearls, two horses and an elephant, richly caparisoned, an inlaid khenjer and sword with a belt for the latter valued at a lakh of rupees. Several trays of jewels were also brought to him; but he took only one string of pearls to which his Majesty added another of great value which he himself had worn.

On the 19th of Shewal, or 19th October,[4] Shah Khorum took his leave of the Emperor, to march to the Dekhan. Amongst other presents, the

[1] R. B. I. 336-7; Iqbal, 89-90; Roe, 258-60.

[2] Roe, 242-4, 256, 274.

[3] R. B. I. 338.

* *Vide* Ayeen Akbery, Vol. I, page 142.

[4] *i.e.*, 8th Aban, only the camp equipage of Khurram left on that day. His leave taking was on the 20th Aban; R. B. I. 337-8.

Emperor gave him a coach, made after the English fashion, and in which he had rode himself.

On the 1st of Zilkadeh, or 30th October, the Emperor set out from Ajmeer for Mendow, in his English coach,[1] drawn by four horses. It is the custom with the kings of Hindostan, when they travel to the east to commence their journey on an elephant; towards the west, on a horse of one colour; towards the north, on a palkee, or singhasen; and towards the south on a carriage. From the time of the Emperor's arrival in Ajmeer to his departure for Mendow, had elapsed three years and five days.[2]

As the route of Shah Khorum lay through the territory of the Ranna, he with his sons came to meet the Prince at Anowleh. His peishkush consisted of a tray of jewels, five elephants, and thirty-seven horses, out of which the Prince accepted one elephant, and three horses. The Ranna and his sons after being honoured with kheluts, took their leave[3]; but his grandson, Jugget Singh, was appointed to attend the Prince on his expedition.

1 Roe, 90, 98, 284, 306; Terry, p. 385; For details of the departure see Roe, 282-7.

* This is the coach which was given to him by Sir Thomas Roe. It is very remarkable that neither Jehangir in his memoirs, nor any eastern historian, has taken any notice of the English ambassador. This must have proceeded from the mean appearance of the embassy; and indeed, Sir Thomas tells us as much in his letter to the Company, dated Ajmeer, 25th January 1615. " But after the English were come away, he, the Emperor asked the Jesuit, whether the King of England was a great king, that sent presents of so small value, and that he looked for some jewels, etc." It is natural to suppose that the Jesuit took advantage of this question to represent the English monarch as a petty Prince of Europe.

2. R. B. I. 340.

3 R. B. I. 344-5.

Before Shah Khorum committed any hostilities in the Dekhan, he sent Rajah Bickermajeet and Adil Khan to Amber, with assurances, that upon peaceably relinquishing all his conquests, he should obtain full pardon; but that if he continued refractory, he should be attacked by a force sufficient to destroy him.

About this time, Jehangir conferred upon Mustefa Khan and his children in Altumgha, the pergunnah of Maldah in Bengal.[1]

A. H. 1026—A. D. 1617.

We must now return to the Dekhan. When Shah Khorum crossed the Nerbudda he was met by the Khankhanan, Khanjehan Khan, Mehabut Khan and all the other principal munsebdars of the army in the Dekhan. He entered Burhanpoor on the 5th of Rubby-ul-Awwel, or 2nd March A. D. 1617, the same day that the Emperor entered the fort of Mendow.[2] At Burhanpoor, Afzul Khan, and Rajah Bickermajeet, joined Shah Khorum, and shortly after, Adil Khan arrived with a considerable peishkush for himself and the other chiefs of the Dekhan. He formally delivered up all the territory of Ballaghaut together with the fort of Ahmednagar.[3] Intelligence hereof was dispatched to the Emperor, and Syed Abdulla Khan, the messenger, carried with him the keys of Ahmednagar. Abdullah Khan obtained the title of Seif

[1] R. B. I. 361.

[2] R. B. I. 368; For description of it see Terry, 181, 183, 184; Finch in Purchas IV. 34-5; Iqbal, 90-7; Firishta, 209-280; Della Valle I. 97.

[3] Price, 198-9; Roe, 340, 385.

Khan,[1] and the Emperor sent the Prince a ruby, taken out of his own diadem.[2] Adil Khan, at the recommendation of Shah Khorum, was honoured with the title of Firzend or son.[3] The peishkush which Adil Khan sent to his Majesty in money, jewels, elephants, and horses, was estimated at fifteen lakhs of rupees; and he bestowed upon Afzul Khan, and Rajah Bickermajeet, two lakhs of rupees each. Rajah Bickermajeet laid out his two lakhs of rupees at Goa, in the purchase of a ruby, which he presented to Shah Khorum.

As soon as Shah Khorum had been every article of the treaty fulfilled, he made preparations for joining the Emperor. He left with the Khan-khanan twenty thousand cavalry, and seven thousand berkundaze infantry; and the rest of his army being twenty-five thousand cavalry,[4] and two thousand berkundaze infantry, accompanied himself to Mendow, where he arrived on the 10th of Shawal,[5] or 30th September 1617.

After the ceremonies of koornish and tesleem, the Emperor descended from the Jarokha, and with his own hands, placed upon the head of Shah Khorum, a tray full of jewels, and another full of gold. The Prince's munseb was now increased to thirty thousand, with the title of Shahjehan,[6] or the king of the world; and in the edict which

[1] R. B. I. 382; Iqbal, 99-101; Khaf. I. 290 1.

[2] *Ibid.*

[3] R. B. I. 387.

[4] 30,000 horses and 7,000 musketeer infantry; R. B. I. 393.

[5] 11th of Shawal according to R. B. I. 393.

[6] R. B. I. 395.

announced his new dignities, it was specified, that he had permission to be seated on a sundely, or chair, in the royal presence.

A few days after his arrival at Court, Shahjehan exposed all his peishkush in the public hall of audience.[1] The Emperor astonished at their magnificence and value, descended from the jarokha to view them more distinctly. Amongst other articles were the following: the ruby which Rajah Bickermajeet bought at Goa for two lakhs of rupees—it weighed seventeen miskals,[2] and the Emperor had not one larger than twelve tanks; an amethyst weighing twenty tanks, valued at a lakh of rupees; a diamond weighing thirty ruttees, valued at forty thousand rupees; another weighing one tank and six ruttees, of the same price; and another weighing one tank valued at thirty thousand rupees; a pearl of sixty-four ruttees, worth twenty-five thousand rupees, two pearls weighing two miskals and eleven ruttees, valued at the same price; one hundred and fifty elephants, three of which had harness and chains of gold, and nine of silver, together with a hundred horses. Besides the above, were rich stuffs, fine linens and other articles to an immense amount. The Emperor accepted of as much as was valued at twenty lakhs of rupees; after which he directed Shahjehan to present Nourjehan Begum, with two lakhs of rupees; and to distribute sixty thousand rupees amongst the other Begums.

[1] R. B. I. 399-401; Iqbal, 105; Khaf, I. 294.

[2] And 5½ surkhs; R. B. I. 400.

Nourjehan Begum gave a grand entertainment in honour of Shahjehan, when she bestowed upon him a khelut, with some valuable jewels, two horses and an elephant. She also made presents to all his officers, who had distinguished themselves during the war. Her expenses on this occasion amounted to three lakhs of rupees.[1]

Ibrahim Khan, the Soobahdar of Bahar, sent the Emperor nine diamonds obtained from the territory of Goorkah, before described; one weighed fourteen and a half tanks, and was valued at a lakh of rupees.[2]

Koteb-ul-Mulk, the Doonyadar or chief of Golconda sent to court a peishkush of fifteen lakhs of rupees, in jewels and other articles.

On the Khankhanan were conferred the governments of Kandeis, Berar and Ahmednagar; and his son Shanowaz Khan was ordered to be stationed at Ballaghaut with twelve thousand cavalry.[3]

A Princess was now born to Shahjehan, by the daughter of Asof Khan and named Roshenrai Begum.

Khandowran, on account of his infirmities, was at his own request removed from the Soobahdary of Cabul to that of Tatah [5]; the former of which was conferred upon Mehabut Khan.

Whilst Jehangir was at Mendow, he was so delighted with Mohammed Niey for his skill in

[1] R. B. I. 397.
[2] R. B. I 379.
[3] R. B. I. 393.
[4] R. B. I. 389.
[5] R. B. I. 397.

singing,[1] that he was ordered to have his weight in silver, which was six thousand and three hundred rupees. After which an elephant was bestowed upon him to carry home himself and the money.[2]

Tobacco, which but a few years before had been brought into Hindostan by the Portuguese, being thought prejudicial to the health of the natives, the Emperor issued an edict prohibiting the use of this plant throughout his dominions: wherein he only followed the example of Shah Abbas, who, on account of its pernicious effects, had forbidden it throughout Persia, under the severest penalties.*[3]

Cossim Khan, Soobahdar of Bengal, being remiss in transmitting his accounts to Court, the Emperor recalled him, and removed Ibrahim Khan from Bahar to Bengal; and Jehangir Kuly Khan succeeded Ibrahim Khan.[4]

Mehabut Khan presented to the Emperor a peishkush, in which was a ruby weighing eleven miskals. When Jehangir was at Ajmeer, a Portuguese merchant asked two lakhs of rupees for this stone, whilst the jewellers valued it at eighty thousand rupees. The same man afterwards carried it to Burhanpoor, where Mehabut Khan bought it for a lakh of rupees.

[1] Playing on the flute.

[2] R. B. I. 376; Price, 199-201.

* The above account of the importation of tobacco into Hindostan, is taken from Jehangir's memoirs; who remarks also, that pine-apples were brought here by the Portuguese and first planted in the royal gardens at Agra, in the commencement of his reign.

[3] R. B. I. 370-1.

[4] R. B. I. 373.

Upon a hunting party Nourjehan Begum killed four tigers with a matchlock, from her elephant. The Emperor was so delighted at her skill, that he made her a present of a pair of emerald bracelets, valued at a lakh of rupees, and bestowed in charity a thousand mohurs.[1]

A. H. 1027—A. D. 1617.

The Emperor was very desirous of enjoying the sport of hunting wild elephants, which he had never yet seen, and having heard great praises of Gujerat, and particularly of the City of Ahmedabad, he resolved to go thither. Added to these inducements for the journey, he wished to have a sight of the ocean, of which he had heard such wonderful relations. Intending to remain at Ahmedabad till after the heat of summer, he sent Miriam-ul-Zemany, and the greatest part of the harem to Agra; after which he set out for Gujerat, along with Nourjehan Begum.[2]

When the Emperor arrived at Cambayet he took up his residence at the garden of Sultan Ahmed, the custom-master of that port. All the ships in the harbour were dressed out; Jehangir embarked on a grab, and sailed in her about two miles.[3] He remained eleven days at Cambayet and then proceeded to Ahmedabad. On the road, he visited the shrine of Shah Alum Bokharee,[4] a very

[1] R. B. I. 375.

[2] R. B. I. 401.

[3] R. B. I. 415.

[4] *Ibid*, 419; Price reverses the order of the march. Ahmedabad (207) being mentioned as the place to which the Emperor went first.

celebrated Mohammedan saint, who is reported to have worked astonishing miracles.

From Mendow to Cambayet is one hundred and twenty-four cose, and from thence to Ahmedabad twenty-one cose. The city did not answer the high expectation which Jehangir had formed, from the descriptions he had heard of it.[1] Although the market places are extensive, yet the shops have a mean appearance, being built of wood and roofed with tiles.

A. H. 1027—A. D. 1618.

Shahjehan now obtained the Soobahdar of Gujerat, in addition to his former jageer.

The Emperor stayed about two months at Ahmedabad, and in the beginning of February set out[2] with intention of proceeding to Agra, by the way of Malwah.

Meer Jemlah, a Persian nobleman, having taken disgust against Shah Abbas, entered into the service of Jehangir, and obtained a munseb of fifteen hundred zat and two hundred cavalry.

On this march, near Malwah, Jehangir shot a lion,[3] which weighed seven maunds and a half. He says in his Toozek, that he had killed many lions, and amongst the rest one at Amda that weighed eight maunds and a half.

In the beginning of March, Jehangir arrived at the town of Sehareh[4] about three cose from

[1] R. B. I. 423-5; Price, 205; Iqbal, 107-8; India of Aurangzeb (trans' by Sarkar), 59-62.

[2] R. B. I. 435, For his dislike of the city on account of its bad climate see B. R. II. 13.

[3] It was a tiger according to R. B. I. 444.

[4] Sajara, R. B. II. 4.

Dehwed, the place where the wild elephants resort and whither he went the next day. The road to it was so overgrown with trees and thickets as to be almost impenetrable. The country people had previously enclosed a spot with nets, and on one side of the enclosure, a platform was erected on the boughs of some trees, for the accommodation of Jehangir, Shahjehan and their suite, which consisted only of a few favourites. Two hundred male elephants, and a number of females, were sent into the enclosure; two men being mounted upon each elephant with ropes and chains. A party of men were now sent to drive the wild elephants into the toil, by the side where the Emperor and Shahjehan were seated. But the jungle was so thick, that the netting could not be properly secured, so that the wild elephants broke through; however, twelve [1] were taken and some of them remarkably fine.

The weather proving very sultry, and many people falling sick, Jehangir thought it would be most prudent to defer his march to Agra, till the end of the rains; and soon after he was confirmed in this resolution, by receiving intelligence that the plague had made its appearance in that quarter. He accordingly returned from Dehwed to Ahmedabad. But the intense heat of the city, and the stagnation of the air, produced a disorder from which few escaped. A fever which lasted two or three days totally exhausted the patient's strength,

[1] 'Although many elephants were not caught at least two excellent ones were captured.' R. B. II., 5

and left pains in all his joints; but the disorder did not prove mortal to any one.[1] The Emperor had a violent attack[2] and was very much reduced by it. The author of the Masir Jehangiry says, it is astonishing how any one could have thought of building a large city on such a spot[3] for that the air is unwholesome, water scarce, and the soil so sandy, that when the wind blows you are almost suffocated with dust; that all the water which can be procured intolerably bad, the wells being brackish, and the tanks frothing with the soap of the washerman; and although the higher ranks of people have cisterns of rain water, yet by being kept from year to year unventilated, it is also very unwholesome. And to complete the unhealthiness of the place, all the neighbouring fields are enclosed with zekoom, which is notorious for occasioning a pestilential atmosphere. Jehangir used to call this city Girdabad, or the city of dust.

On the 22nd of Ramzan, or 1st September 1618, the Emperor marched from Ahmednagar for Agra.[4]

On the 16th of the month of Dey,[5] or December 26th, about an hour and twelve minutes before sunrise, there appeared on the horizon a luminous little cloud; it rose later every morning twenty-four minutes, till on the sixteenth morning it was

[1] R. B. II., 10, 13, 14; Khaf. I., 294; Terry, 226-7

[2] R. B. II., 12; Roe 473n

[3] Also R. B. II., 13

[4] Ahmadabad? R.B. II., 25; Roe, 482n

[5] Aban according to the Tuzuk.

discovered to be a comet with a dark tail.[1] Its course was from the sign of Scorpio to Libra. It was generally believed to have occasioned the plague, as well as to have prognosticated the war between the Emperor and Shahjehan, which for seven years so deluged the empire with blood, that there was hardly a family but shared in the calamity.

About the same time, at Kandahar, there appeared suddenly a swarm of rats, which entirely destroyed the fruits of the earth and devoured all the grain that was in store. Great numbers were killed and the remainder vanished, as suddenly as they had appeared.[2]

On the 15th Zilkadeh, or 23rd October, whilst the Emperor was at Dehwed, the daughter of Asaf Khan brought Shahjehan a son, whom Jehangir named Aurungzebe.[3] When the army arrived at the city of Oujein, Shahjehan celebrated the birth of the young prince, with great magnificence.[4]

When the Emperor arrived on the borders of the Ranna's territory, Kurren came out to meet him, and congratulated him upon the conquest of the Dekhan.[5]

Morteza Khan, who was now besieging Kengerah,[6] found out that Rajah Soorej Mull was engaged in a treasonable correspondence with the enemy. He advised the Emperor of the discovery;

---

[1] R.B. II., 48 ; E.D. VI, 363 ; Iqbal, 117. Sixteen nights after this phenomenon a star showed itself in the same quarter. Its head was luminous but not its tail.
[2] R.B. II., 49
[3] R.B. II., 47
[4] R.B. II., 50
[5] R.B. II., 54
[6] R.B. II., 223-4; Khaf I., 306-7

but the artful Rajah wrote to Shahjehan that the whole was a forgery of Morteza Khan to ruin him, and he had such credit with the Prince, that he obtained permission to come to court, to exculpate himself. At this time, Morteza Khan happening to die, the operations against Kengerah were for some time suspended. Soorej Mull having persuaded Shahjehan of his innocence, accompanied him to the Dekhan and there behaved so well, that upon peace being restored to that quarter, he was sent to conduct the siege of Kengerah; but much against the Emperor's judgment, who thought it imprudent to trust, with such an important command, a man accused of treachery: his arguments so far prevailed with Shahjehan that he sent along with him his own Bukhshee Mohamed Tuckee, [Taqi] to watch his actions. But no sooner were they arrived before the place, then he quarrelled with Mohamed Tuckee, and by artful representations obtained his recall, and Bickermajeet, with a considerable reinforcement was ordered there in his stead. But before his arrival at Kengerah, Soorej Mull had disbanded a considerable part of the army, when he and his party fell upon[2] the rest, plundered and slaughtered them, and then seized some pergunnahs at the foot of the mountains, belonging to the jageer of Etemadeddowlah.[3]

The 20th of the month of Dey, or 30th December 1618, the Emperor encamped at the tank

[1] R.B. II., 55
[2] Rose in revolt.
[3] R. B. II., 54-7

of Futtehpoor.[1] The tank was measured and found to be seven cose in circuit.

The city of Agra not being yet free from the infection of the plague,[2] Jehangir continued some time at Futtehpoor. He visited the tomb of Sheikh Sileem Chiesty[3] which has a beautiful mosque of stone, built by order of Akber, in the erection of which were expended five lakhs of rupees.

When Bickermajeet arrived in Punjab, Soorej Mull demanded a parley, which was peremptorily refused. He was soon driven from the forts of Mend and Mekran, and in retreating, lost many of his men; at length he was totally dispossessed of the lands, which had been held by his ancestors for many generations, and it was with difficulty that he escaped with his life.[4]

In the latter end of this year, there appeared in Cashmeer, a dreadful disorder, which proved fatal to great numbers. The patient was seized with a headache and bleeding at the nose, and died the next day. In whatever house, this disorder appeared, it carried off the whole family.

A. H. 1028—A. D. 1619

The Emperor celebrated the new year at Futtehpoor and during this festival honoured Shahjehan with a visit, who presented a nuzzar of

---

1 R. B. II., 64, 66
2 R. B. II., 65, 66; Roe, 268, 312, 326n, 327, 328, 334n, 336; Eng. Factories in India, E. D. VI, 407, p. 82
3 R. and B. II., 70-2; Price, 209
4 R. B. II., 74

jewels and other articles to the value of five lakhs of rupees.[1]

About this time Mocurreb Khan was appointed Soobhadar of Bahar;[2] and Sirdar Khan obtained a jageer in Mongheer, with the feudatory of Tirhoot.

On the fourth of Jemady ul Awwel or April 8th, Jehangir entered the city of Agra,[3] where Sultan Purveiz paid him his respects,[4] having just arrived from Allahabad.

About this time died Shahnowaz Khan,[5] the son of the Khankhanan. He was a gallant officer, but killed himself by excessive drinking.

Khandowran Shah Beg Khan, worn out with age, obtained the Emperor's permission to resign the Government of Tatah, and in reward for his eminent services, the pergunnah of Khooshab in Punjab, yielding seventy-five thousand rupees per annum was conferred upon him in jageer.[6]

His Majesty ordered obelisks to be erected at the distance of every cose on the high road from Agra to Lahore: at every third obelisk a well was sunk, and each side of the road was planted with trees, for the refreshment of travellers.[7]

After remaining five months at Agra, the Emperor set out for Cashmeer, leaving the fort of Agra under the command of Lushker Khan.[8] When he arrived at Mehtra, Sultan Purveiz took his

[1] R. B. II., 78-9
[2] R. B. II., 89
[3] R. B. II., 84-5
[4] Price, 213-16
[5] R. B. II., 87
[6] R. B. II., 97; and his sons were well provided for.
[7] R. B. II., 100
[8] R. B. II., 102; Price 226

leave,[1] and departed for Allahabad, where his jageer was situated.

A. H. 1029—A. D. 1619

Khan Alum now returning from his embassy to the Court of Persia, the Emperor went out to meet him from the garden of Kelanore. He had long treated him with familiar intimacy, and used to go to his house without any ceremony. Among the presents from Shah Abbass, was a picture of Timour's victory over Towk Tomish Khan. It contained two hundred and forty portraits, amongst which were most of Timour's relations. The painter's name is Keleel Mirza Sharokhoe.[2]

Through the management of Khan Azem, a Sonassee fakir, named Atcher Roop, interceded with the Emperor for Sultan Khusru, and obtained his pardon, with permission to come to Court.[3]

About this time Cushtwar, situated to the north of Cashmeer, was conquered by Dilawer Khan, the Soobahdar.[4] The Emperor rewarded him with one year's revenue of that territory.

A. H. 1029—A. D. 1620

The road to Peerpunchal was difficult to pass at this season of the year on account of the depth of the snow; but being the nearest way and as the Emperor was desirous of arriving at Cashmeer during the spring, he and the rest of the harem, along with Elemadeddowlah at Rhotass till the melting of the snow; whilst Mirza Rustam

[1] R. B. II., 107
[2] R. B. II., 115-16
[3] R. B. II., 107; Price, 216-19 gives a very interesting account of the release which lacks corroboration.
[4] R. B. II., 122, 135-40

and Khan Azem went on with a party by the road of Poontch.[1] On the road, Jehangir received intelligence of the death of Ranna Amer Singh,[2] upon which he dispatched Kishendoss to invest Kurren with the title of Ranna and he was confirmed in all the possessions enjoyed by his father.

When the Emperor arrived at Puckelee,[3] he sent Mehabut Khan to command an expedition against the Afghans of Bungish. The mountains of Puckelee are enamelled with flowers, amongst which are violets, equal in fragrance to those cultivated in gardens, but of a fainter colour. The next day it rained and snowed, which made the road so slippery that many of the baggage elephants fell down the side of the mountains and were killed; of those that perished thus, were twenty-five belonging to the Emperor. They were obliged to halt two days at Puckelee. The next day's march they met with peach and apricot trees in full blossom. Sircar Puckelee[4] is thirty-five cose in length, and twenty-five in breadth. On the west are the mountains of Cashmeer, on the north the mountains of Kuttore, and on the south the mountains of Poontch. He crossed the bridge over the river Nainsook which takes its rise in the pass between Badakhshan and Tibbet. Two new bridges were erected for the army to cross over, each measuring eighteen yards in length: the

[1] R. B. II., 123
[2] R. B. II., 123
[3] This is not right. It must be Malgalli; R. B. II., 124n
[4] R. B. II., 126-7

elephants swam over. He encamped on the banks of the river Kishengung. Near this place is a level spot about fifty yards square, where he celebrated the festival of the new year. He was here overtaken by Shahjehan, who had made an excursion to see the City of Lahore.[1] The whole of the road from Kishengung to Cashmeer is by the side of the river Behut. You go over very high mountains, from some of which issue rapid cataracts. This road being narrow and difficult to pass, only Nourjehan Begum, Shahjehan, Asof Khan and a few others were allowed to accompany the Emperor; Khusru and the rest being ordered to keep a day's march behind.[2] The first day they were overtaken by a violent thunder storm and obliged to take shelter in a tent which luckily had been pitched by Motamid Khan at Bhelbass.[3] At the next stage Kha-ey, the Emperor, made Motamid Khan a present of a complete suit of clothes which he had worn himself, and promoted him to a munseb of one thousand five hundred zat and five hundred cavalry.[4] After passing the hills, they descended into a delightful valley enamelled with flowers, and proceeded with the village of Syar. To add to the beauty of the scene, here is a prodigious fine water-fall. The next stage was Barahmoolah on the banks of the Behut, and here are many pleasant seats built by the merchants of Serrynagur who attended the Emperor from hence

[1] Price, 240
[2] R. B. II., 131
[3] Price, 241
[4] R. B. II., 132.

in their boats. Here he found Dilawer Khan, Soobahdar of Cashmeer, who was just returned from Cushtwar.[1] This territory which was then newly acquired, is sixty cose from Cashmeer: the revenue is estimated at a lakh of rupees. In the beginning of April, Jehangir entered his new palace near the tank of Dull. Here is a strong stone fort began in the time of Akber, and finished in the present reign. The next day Dilawer Khan brought in chains the Rajah of Cushtwar, who was informed that if he would leave his sons at court as hostages for his future good conduct, he should be set at liberty, and that unless he gave such security he should be committed to one of the fortresses of Hindostan: he consented to the requisition. Jehangir, after passing three days at his new palace, entered Serrynagur, the capital city of Cashmeer. Its longitude is 105 degrees and latitude 35 degrees.

Mohammedanism first appeared in Cashmeer about the commencement of the eighth century of the Hegira; and in 772 of the same era, or A. D. 1370, Meer Syed Aly Hamadany went thither and gained many proselytes. In A. H. 994 or A. D. 1585, the whole subah was conquered. Sheikh Abulfazel in his Akbernamah, has computed Cashmeer to be in length 120 cose, and in breadth from 10 to 25 cose. Jehangir ordered an actual measurement to be made, when it was found to be sixty-six cose long and from ten to twenty-seven cose broad.[2]

---

[1] R. B. II., 139-40

[2] R. B. II., 140-1

The Khankhanan now sent the Emperor intelligence of the revolt of Nizam-ul-Mulk, and other chiefs in the Dekhan, who after possessing themselves of some of the dependencies of Ballakhaut and Berar, had now besieged the fort of Ahmednagar. A supply of twenty lakhs of rupees was ordered to be sent from Agra to the Khankhanan.[1]

About this time, Mehabut Khan gained a considerable victory over the Afghans of the territory of Bungish.

Dilawer Khan dying in his government of Cashmeer,[2] Eradut Khan was appointed to succeed him.[3] About the same time died Khandowran, in the ninetieth year of his age.[4] He was a native of Mehawer'lnehr, and came into Hindostan in the service of Mirza Hakeem brother of the Emperor Akber. He was possessed of integrity, valour and liberality in an eminent degree.[5]

Jehangir was now, for the first time, attacked with an asthma,[6] which annually returned upon him with increased violence, till it terminated his existence.

In the month of October, Jehangir set out for Punjab, and in November arrived at Lahore[7] where he resided at a new palace on which was expended seven lakhs of rupees.

---

[1] R. B. II., 155-6
[2] R. B. II., 167
[3] R. B. II., 175
[4] R. B. II., 172
[5] And the. Tuzuk says, he performed great services for the dynasty; R. B. II., 172
[6] R, B. II., 12-13; 35; 176
[7] R. B. II., 183.

It had been a practice in Rajore, for the widows of Mohammedans to bury themselves alive with their husbands, in emulation of the Hindu wives, who, on the like occasion, devote themselves to flames. Just before Jehangir arrived there, a girl of twelve years of age having buried herself in this manner, he prohibited the barbarous custom; and threatened with death every one who should be found guilty of partaking in the crime.[1]

A. H. 1030—A. D. 1620

On the 1st of Moherrem, or the 15th of November, the fort of Kengerah surrendered to Rajah Bickermajeet. It is situated in the mountains south of Lahore and had hitherto been deemed impregnable, never having before been in the possession of any Mohammedan prince.[2]

When Dilawer Khan came to Cashmeer, to pay his respects to the Emperor, he left the territory of Cushtwar under charge of Nasser-ullah Arab, who imprudently giving part of his troops leave of absence, at the same time that he ill-treated the natives, they rose upon him, massacred his remaining force, and made him prisoner. The Emperor now sent Jilal, son of the late Dilawer Khan to reduce the country again to obedience.[3]

Adil Khan, Nizam-ul-Mulk, and Koteb-ul-Mulk, having entered into a confederacy, collected together an army of sixty thousand cavalry

[1] R. B. II., 181
[2] R. B. II., 183 ; Khaf I., 306-7 ; E. D. VI., 525-6, 527-33.
[3] R. B. II., 170-1

with which they conquered the whole territory of Ballaghaut. The imperial troops retreated to Mekher, and kept skirmishing with the enemy for three months, when their supplies being cut off, they were obliged to descend from the mountains and encamp at Balapoor; but neither finding any relief at that place, they retreated to the Khan-khanan at Burhanpoor, whither the enemy followed, and laid siege to that fortress.[1] The Emperor sensible of the ill effects of remaining at such distance from the capital, resolved to return to Agra, and to send Shahjehan again into the Dekhan. Shahjehan's army was now appointed to consist of six hundred and fifty munsebdars, one thousand Ahdees, one thousand Turkish cavalry armed with matchlocks, five thousand men for the service of the artillery,[2] and thirty-one thousand Hindostan cavalry, with a supply of a crore of rupees.[3] It was determined that Khusru should go into the Dekhan with Shahjehan, who should have discretionary orders to treat him in any manner he might think proper. Motamid Khan accompanied Shahjehan[4] and Khanjehan Khan was appointed subahdar of Multan.

A. H. 1030—A. D. 1621

The same day that Shahjehan marched for the Dekhan, Jehangir set out for Agra. In January he left Delhi, visited the shrine of Humayun[5] and reached Agra in March.

[1] R. B. II., 188-90
[2] R. B. II., 190 gives 1000 in the text
[3] R. B. II., 190
[4] R. B. II., 192
[5] R. B. II., 196-7

When the Emperor was last at Agra, Shah Abbass sent him a ruby which had descended from Ulugh Beg to the Seffy Family. On it was originally engraved in the Nuskh character, *Ulugh Beg, son of Sharokh Bahadre, son of Emir Timour Goorgan.* To which was added, by the order of Shah Abbass in Nustalikh, *Shah Abbass, the slave of Shah Wallayet,* or the *king of sanctity* (Aly). The Emperor was mightily pleased at receiving such a relic of his ancestor; and in addition to the former inscriptions, ordered the following to be engraved: JEHANGIR SHAH, AKBER SHAH, A. H. 1028.[1]

Shahzadeh Sheriar was now promoted to a munseb of eight thousand zat, and four thousand cavalry; and shortly after married a daughter of Nourjehan Begum by Shere Afkun.[2]

When Shahjehan arrived on the banks of the river Chembel, he entered the thirtieth year of his age, and was weighed with the usual ceremonies. At the time Hymayun[3] went upon an expedition against Ranna Sanka, he made a vow, that if he gained a victory over the infidels, he would ever after abstain entirely from the use of wine. Shahjehan was determined to excel his grand-father, (ancestor) by making an offering previous to the victory. He accordingly ordered that all the wine in the camp should immediately be started into the river, and the drinking vessels of gold and silver, as well as those inlaid with precious stones, were

[1] R. B. II., 195
[2] R. B. II., 187, 202
[3] This is evidently a mistake for the story is told of Babur.

broken to pieces in his presence and distributed in charity. At Owjein he was met by Mohammed Tuckee, killadar of Mendow, who informed him that the enemy having crossed the Nerbudda, had set fire to the suburbs of Mendow. Shahjehan immediately sent off two detachments, one commanded by Khojeh Abdul Hassan, and the other by Byram Beg. Being joined by Mohammed Tuckee with a considerable reinforcement from the fort they arrived on the banks of the Nerbudda in the morning, and attacked the enemy, who after suffering great slaughter fled without stopping, till they joined the army before Burhanpoor. Shahjehan sent orders to his generals not to cross the Nerbudda till he could join them. [1]

Notwithstanding the approach of Shahjehan, the siege of Burhanpoor was not raised, but the Khankhanan contrived to elude the vigilance of the besiegers, and joined Shahjehan at Mendow. Shahjehan remained nine days at Mendow, to refresh his men and collect sufficient stock of grain for the next campaign. He bestowed thirty lakhs of rupees upon the jageerdars, to make them amends for the losses they had sustained from the ravage and devastation of the enemy. He then formed five divisions, each consisting of six thousand cavalry, and appointed for them the following commanders: Abdullah Khan, Darab Khan, Khojeh Abdul Hassan, Rajah Bickermajeet, and Rajah Bheem. Darab Khan was nominally the commander-in-chief, but

[1] R. B. II., 206.

Shahjehan placed the most reliance upon Bickermajeet. These united forces drove the enemy from Burhanpoor with great slaughter and then follwed for eight days to Kehrkee, the residence of Nizam-ul-Mulk, and his prime minister Amber; but a day before their arrival there, Nizam-ul-Mulk and his family retired to Dowletabad, and Amber took post at the foot of the mountains with his front secured by a swamp. The imperial troops entered Kehrkee, and levelled with the ground the magnificent buildings which Nizam-ul-Mulk had been twenty years erecting at an incredible expense.

Shahjehan left a garrison in Kehrkee, and then marched to the relief of Ahmednagar. Amber, alarmed at the rapid progress of the imperial arms, when Shahjehan arrived at Putten, sent a messenger to him, with a promise to remove immediately from Ahmednagar, abandon all his conquests and make the most ample submissions to the Emperor. Shahjehan insisted that Nizam-ul-Mulk should resign to the Emperor that part of his country which remained unconquered at the conclusion of the last war; and that Adil Khan, Nizam-ul-Mulk, and Koteb-ul-Mulk should together pay a peishkush of fifty lakhs of rupees. Amber readily acceded to these terms; he immediately raised the siege of Ahmednagar and his troops joined Shahjehan at Terminee. In consideration of this victory, Shahjehan ordered a stone-fort to be built to which he gave the name of Zufferabad.[1] He stationed

[1] Or the city of Victory.

garrisons throughout the Dekhan; and during the rains cantoned his army at Zufferabad. He consented to receive the peishkush half in money and half in goods in the following proportions: from Adil Khan eighteen lakhs, from Nizam-ul-Mulk twelve lakhs and from Koteb-ul-Mulk twenty lakhs. Affairs in the Dekhan were now completely settled; and after the rains Shahjehan marched with his army to Burhanpoor.[1]

Afzul Khan who was sent to the Emperor with intelligence of Shahjehan's great success, was rewarded with considerable presents, and Jehangir amongst other things sent to his victorious son the family ruby, which he had himself received from Shah Abbass.[2]

When the two Persian Ambassadors took their leave, the Emperor gave to one a present of forty thousand, and to the other thirty thousand rupees in money, besides khelaats and other articles to a considerable amount. The presents for Shah Abbass were of great value.

Jilal, son of the late Dilawer Khan, making no progress in Cushwar, Eradut Khan, the subahdar of Cashmeer, was ordered thither, and after having entirely subdued the country, he placed strong garrisons in different places.[3]

About this time Housheng, the nephew of Khan Alum the Emperor's great favourite, having committed murder, was executed for it.[4]

---

1 R. B. II., 206-8; Iqbal 182-4; Khaf I., 314
2 R. B. II., 208-11
3 R. B. II., 210
4 R. B. II., 211

The Emperor had now another alarming attack of Asthma,[1] on which occasion Purveiz hastened from Patna to Agra[2]; but before his arrival Jehangir was out of danger.

Abdullah Khan having left the Dekhan without permission of Shahjehan, the Emperor deprived him of his jageer, and Etemad Roy was ordered to conduct him back to the prince.[3]

The intense heat of Agra being unfavourable to Jehangir's complaint, he set out in November for the northern mountains, determined if he found that climate agree with him, to build a city there on the banks of the Ganges, for his summer retreat, or else to proceed to Cashmeer.[4]

When Jehangir arrived at Phorloon, one of the dependencies of Seena, he and Nourjehan Begum, with a small party, set out to free the fort of Kengerah: Etemadeddowlah was at this time very ill, and the accounts of next morning were so unfavourable, that the Emperor and Nourjehan Begum returned the ensuing evening to the camp, where they found him in great danger. He fainted frequently and appeared so totally exhausted, that Nourjehan doubted whether he was sensible, and pointing to the Emperor, asked her father whether he knew him when he repeated the following lines from Anveri:

"IF A PERSON WHO WAS BORN BLIND WERE TO COME INTO HIS PRESENCE,

[1] R. B. II., 212
[2] R. B. II., 215
[3] R. B. II., 217
[4] R. B. II., 217

HE WOULD DISCOVER NOBILITY UPON THAT FOREHEAD WHICH ENLIGHTENS THE WORLD."

The Emperor stayed by his pillow several[1] hours, after which he became senseless and expired the next morning.[2] This great minister was endowed with such superior abilities that the Emperor could not reasonably be blamed for the confidence he reposed in him. His corpse was conducted to Agra by his son Etekad Khan, and interned in the vizier's own garden.

Two days after the death of Etemadeddowlah the Emperor and the Begum recommenced their journey to Kengerah and after travelling four days encamped on the banks of the Bain Gungah. The next day, the Emperor entered the fort of Kengerah. It is surprisingly strong, being fortified with twenty-three bastions. It measures within side above a cose in length, and from fifteen to twenty-two tenabs in breadth, and it is one hundred and fourteen yards high. In it are two large reservoirs of water. When the Emperor had walked over the whole fort, he visited the temple of Durgah, called Behwen, in its neighbourhood. Near this temple, at the foot of the mountain, is a volcano that emits flames continually, and the natives who call it JOWELAH MOOKHEE believe it to be the miraculous production of one of their idols.[3]

---

[1] R.B. II., 222 says, he stayed there for two hours.
[2] His wife had passed away earlier, *i.e.*, in 1621. He died at the end of January 1622.
[3] R B. II, 223-4

The Emperor bestowed upon Nourjehan Begum the sole possession of all her father's property of every description, with the same jageers and distinctions that he had enjoyed.[1] Her eldest brother Abdul Hassan, was appointed to the office of principal Dewan.

In the latter end of this year, Sultan Khusru died at Burhanpoor of the cholick.[2]

A. H. 1031—A. D. 1621

Mehabut Khan met the Emperor at Baba Hassan Abdal, and when the army encamped at Puckelee, returned to Cabul his subahdary loaded with favours.[3]

When Jehangir arrived at Cashmeer, he issued an edict forbidding the levying of an oppressive tax, under the name of Russoom Foujdary.[4]

The Emperor having suffered himself to be lulled into security by the warm professions of inviolable friendship, so repeatedly tendered to him by Shah Abbass, has lately kept but a small garrison[5] in the important fortress of Kandahar, which offered such a temptation to the Persian monarch as he was not able to resist; he suddenly brought a large army against it, and Abdalazeez Khan, the Governor, having no force capable of making resistance against such a mighty attack, surren-

---

1 R.B. II., 228

2 R.B. II., 228. Beveridge in J.R.A.S. 1907, p 599 sees no evidence of Khusru having been poisoned or strangled. Khafikhan, De Laet, the English Factors, Della Valle [I. 58], Peter Mundy [II. 104-5], Terry 412; Pelsart, Herbert, Von Posar and the Rajput chronicles charge Khurram with murdering Khusru.

3 R.B. II., 231

4 R. B., II, 232

5 300 or 400 soldiers. R. B. II.,230.

dered the place.[1] The Emperor wrote immediately to Shahjehan, and in his letter returned thanks to God, that the success of his son's arms in the Dekhan would now allow him to march against Kandahar, to wipe off the disgrace which the Empire had suffered by the capture of that fortress.

A few months after this despatch, Zeimul Abedeen arrived at Court, from Shahjehan, with advice of his arrival at Mendow, from whence after recruiting his army, he intended to proceed to Malwah, to continue there during the rains, and upon the breaking up of the monsoon march to the siege of Kandahar.[2] He wrote the Emperor that he did not require any reinforcements, but that in order to ensure success, it would be necessary for him to be vested with the full command of the army, without being subject to any control. He requested that on account of its vicinity to Kandahar, the subah of Punjab might be given him in jageer, with the fort of Runthore as a place of safety for his family.

A. H. 1031—A. D. 1622

During the administration of Etemadeddowlah, the ambitious views of the Begum were under some degree of restraint; but immediately upon the death of her worthy father, her influence and authority became intolerable; to Jehangir nothing was left but the empty name of Emperor, whilst all the arrangements of Government were solely managed by her; so that advancement and degrada-

---

[1] R. B. II., 233
[2] R. B. II., 234

tion were the effects of her caprice or resentment. She was alarmed at the rapid decline of the Emperor's health, being sensible that if after his death Shahjehan should ascend the throne, she must sink into insignificance. She therefore now began to concert measures for frustrating his views and to secure the continuance of her own unlimited dominion. For the attainment of these ends, she fixed her eyes upon Sheriar, and resolved to raise him to the empire, confident that from his weak capacity he would be the mere pageant of a king, whom she could manage at her pleasure; and she doubted not but a liberal distribution of the public treasure would effectually support his pretensions to the succession. In order to advance her schemes with the Emperor she took every opportunity to insinuate into his mind unfavourable sentiments of Shahjehan. She said it was evident, from the terms of his letter, that he only wanted to be invested with absolute power to dethrone his father. Her creatures were industrious in improving upon her base suggestions, till at length the Emperor was perfectly persuaded of their reality. When she had gained thus far upon his credibility, she offered to be at the sole expense of the operations against Kandahar, and entreated that Sheriar might be invested with the command, under the tuition of Mirza Rustam, who from having been many years governor of that province, would be able to afford him the best advice. She added that she would cheerfully expend in this service all that she inherited from her father, with whatever else she had acquired through his Majesty's favour and indulgence, and which would be found fully adequate to the maintenance of an army requisite for so great an enterprise. But she required that Shahjehan's jageers in Agra, Ajmeer and Lahore should be transferred to Sheriar, and that the former should receive equivalents in the Dekhan, Malwah and Gujerat. The infatuated Jehangir complied with all her demands; Shahjehan was dispossessed of his jageers which were conferred upon Sheriar, and the former was directed to send all his troops to court, and remain alone in the Dekhan. Officers were appointed to see these arrangements carried into immediate execution, and Abdal Selam, Shahjehan's resident at court, was sent to communicate these orders to his master. Sheriar was promoted to the rank of twelve thousand zat and eight thousand cavalry and appointed commander-in-chief of the intended expedition against Kandahar.[1] Mirza Rustam being made Etaleek to Sheriar, and commander-in-chief of his troops, was sent forward to Lahore, to make the necessary preparations. Just about the time that the jageers were transferred to Sheriar, Shahjehan, ignorant of his disgrace at court, had written a letter to the Emperor, requesting that the pergunnah of Dholpoor might be added to his jageer; and confident of the Emperor's compliance, had sent Derya Khan to take charge of it; but Shereef-ul-Mulk having repaired thither on the part of

[1] R.B. II., 237

Sheriar, a skirmish ensued, in which Shereef lost one of his eyes by an arrow. This event served to increase the Emperor's suspicions, as well as to inflame the Begum's resentment against Shahjehan.[1]

In July the Emperor proceeded on his march from Lahore, and in September crossed the Chenab, where he was met by Mirza Rustam. At the same place arrived Afzul Khan, with a letter from Shahjehan, wherein he expostulated with his father in the most respectful and pathetic terms.[2] After expatiating upon the dutiful tenor of his whole life, he modestly mentioned the services he had so recently performed, lamented that he should have forfeited his Majesty's parental regard, without the shadow of offence, for the gratification of the ambition of a base woman, and her degenerate son-in-law. He implored the Emperor to do him only common justice; but declared that whilst he was so unfortunate as to labour under his royal displeasure, so far from desiring to receive any equivalent for the jageers of which he had been so disgracefully bereft, he only begged leave to retire to Surat, which might be considered as the door to the house of righteousness (Mecca) where he would employ his whole time in praying for his Majesty's health and prosperity. He conjured the Emperor to consult his own better judgment, and not suffer himself to be misled by the artful and weak counsels of the

[1] R. B. II., 235-6
[2] R. B. II., 238-9

Begum, which, if pursued, must occasion his own dishonour and destruction, and terminate in the utter ruin of the empire.

Jehangir was fully sensible of the truth of Shahjehan's representations and endeavoured to convince the Begum of their propriety, setting forth to her the injustice of dispossessing him of his jageers, without being able to assign any reason for so extraordinary a conduct. But the Begum's resolutions were not to be altered by arguments, however founded on reason, justice or humanity; and her influence over the Emperor, was now so absolute, that she prevailed upon him to commit a farther injury by despoiling his son of his remaining jageers in Hissar and Duab, which like the rest were assigned over to Sheriar. Orders to this effect were issued to the Dewans. In the imperial mandate which conveyed these commands to Shahjehan, he was desired to satisfy himself by taking in exchange any parts of the Dekhan, Malwah and Gujerat, that he might prefer, and had permission to reside at any of those places; at the same time he was commanded to send away the troops that were required for the siege of Kandahar.[1] Afzul Khan boldly protested against these iniquitous proceedings, but was obliged to return to Shahjehan without effecting anything.[2] By these violent measures, the Begum meant to try Shahjehan's disposition and to bring matters to a

[1] R. B. II., 239.

[2] Iqbal 194, 196 says that Nur Jahan would not permit Afzal Khan to have audience of the Emperor; R. B. II, 23-9; Khaf. I, 332.

speedy crisis. Should he tamely submit to this shameful treatment, she gained her ends at once without further trouble or opposition; and if on the other hand he was driven into open rebellion, he would incur the odium of commencing an unnatural war, in which by means of her resources she hoped to be able to crush him. In short Shahjehan wished to proceed by mild and lenient measures so as to avoid the appearance of disobedience on his part; whilst, on the contrary, the views of the Begum were to create an irreconcileable jealousy between the Emperor and Shahjehan and raise the fortune of Sheriar upon the ruin of the latter. Her brother, Asof Khan was known to be well disposed towards Shahjehan; but whenever the present transactions became the subject of conversation, he had the prudence to observe a strict silence. The Begum now finding no opposition to her will, threw off the mask and made no secret of her intentions. Mehabut Khan, who was dissatisfied with Shahjehan, and who both hated and envied Asof Khan, was ordered to court from his government of Cabul. Although the letter bore the seal of the Begum, yet Mehabut Khan not being able to persuade himself that such an entire change of measures could so suddenly have taken place, suspected to be the artifice of Asof Khan to draw him to court, for the purpose of sacrificing him to his revenge. He therefore wrote in answer to the Begum, that as long as Asof Khan remained at court, he dared not obey her summons, and that therefore, if she really wished to avail herself of his services, she must first send her brother to Bengal and destroy Motamid Khan.

The munseb of Mehabut Khan was immediately raised to six thousand zat and the like number of cavalry, and his son Amanullah Khan was nominated to the rank of three thousand zat and one thousand seven hundred cavalry, and appointed acting Subahdar of Cabul, whilst his father should remain at court. Asof Khan was despatched to Agra for the royal treasure, that had been amassing there from the commencement of the reign of Akber. But this was only a pretence to get him out of the way, in order to dispel the apprehensions of Mehabut Khan, and that he might not be a spy upon the actions of the Begum and her party.

Abdullah Khan from Culpee, and Khanjehan Khan from Multan,[1] now paid their respects to the Emperor, and Mirza Khan, the son of the former, obtained in marriage a daughter of the late Sultan Daniel. Khanjehan presented the Emperor with a peishkush of a thousand Irakee horses.

Hyder Beg, ambassador from Shah Abbass arrived now at Lahore, with a letter from Jehangir, full of declarations of friendship; he received a khelut, but was ordered to depart immediately.

Some very harsh expressions having fallen from Shahjehan, upon the receipt of the royal mandate, and which was reported to the Emperor, he became much alarmed at what might be the

[1] R. B. II., 247.

consequence of driving his son to despair, and employed Moussavee Khan, a man of great sagacity, to go to the Prince, under the pretence of giving good advice, but in fact to penetrate into his designs, that measures might be adopted accordingly.[1]

When Mehabut Khan arrived at Lahore, he assured Jehangir that unless Motamid Khan was destroyed, it would be impossible to concert any measures with such secrecy as to elude his penetration; and added, that if the Emperor was in the least scrupulous about ordering his execution, he need only send him to Cabul on pretence of business, when Mehabut Khan would take care to have him despatched on the road.

A letter was now received from Etebar Khan, the killadar of Agra, with advice that Shahjehân had marched from Mendow, at the head of a large army; but that his intentions were yet unknown.[2]

When Afzul Khan returned to the Dekhan, and communicated to Shahjehan all the particulars of his father's behaviour, with the wicked designs of the Begum and her party, he assured him that matters were now come to a crisis, when remonstrances would have no avail, and that abject submissions must terminate in utter destruction: that in the same manner as he had been dispossessed of his jageers in Hindostan, he would gradually be deprived of those in Malwah, Gujerat and the Dekhan; and when thus bereft of every

[1] R.B. II., 246.
[2] R. B. II., 247.

resource, he would be crushed without having the power to make any resistance. Shahjehan, convinced of the truth of these arguments, resolved to act with vigour and accordingly without loss of time marched his army towards Agra.[1]

As soon as the Emperor received certain intelligence that Shahjehan was marching towards Agra, Mehabut Khan and the Begum inflamed his mind against his son, and precipitated him into violent measures. It was agreed, that the Emperor, under pretence of hunting, should proceed to the river at Sultanpoor in Punjab,[2] and there wait till it could be ascertained whether Shahjehan was coming in a hostile or peaceable manner; that if his intentions were discovered to be inimical, the Emperor should cross the river and oppose him; but if he should not commit any act of hostility, measures suitable to the occasion might be pursued. Having thus formed a plan of operations, the Emperor marched from Lahore in the beginning of February. Daily advices were received from Etebar Khan of the rapid advances of Shahjehan towards Agra. Etebar Khan did not think it safe to remove the treasure [3]; Asof Khan concurred with him in his opinion, and prepared to join the Emperor.

A. H. 1032.—A. D. 1623.

Upon receiving the above advices, the Emperor crossed the river at Sultanpoor, and proceeded towards Delhi. Thus, by the wicked intrigues of

[1] R. B. II., 249.
[2] R. B. II., 248.
[3] R. B. II., 247-8.

the Begum, the whole empire was in a flame. A dutiful son was compelled for his own preservation, to take arms against an affectionate parent. The situation of the Emperor was truly deplorable; in the decline of life, and whilst labouring under a grievous bodily infirmity, to be forced into a climate inimical to his disorder, in order to conduct an unnatural war, which must in its consequences prove injurious to both parties on whichsoever side victory might declare. It was moreover a lamentable reflection, that those very troops, with their general, who had gained so many victories over the enemies of the empire, should now sheath their swords in the very vitals of their country.

Mehram Khan, one of the eunuchs of the Serai, together with Kheleel Beg, Fidaiy Khan, and Motamid Khan, being accused at this time of holding a secret correspondence with Shahjehan, were apprehended, and upon the evidence of Mirza Rustam, who bore an inveterate enmity against Kheleel and another suborned witness who swore against Mehram Khan, they were both put to death ; Fidaiy Khan, fully exculpated himself and was pardoned,[1] but Motamid Khan was dismissed from the service, and banished to Tatah.[2]

Mousavee Khan met Shahjehan at Futtehpoor, and was received in the most gracious manner.[3] The prince agreed to send with him Cazy Abdulazeez, to assure the Emperor, that he only wished

[1] And promoted. R.B. II., 249.
[2] R.B. II., 249 ; Iqbal, 199.
[3] R.B. II., 249.

to come to a personal explanation; from his conviction that from the intrigues of the Begum, no negotiation could be managed through any medium, and that he earnestly desired to have an interview with his Majesty, before matters were carried to extremity.

Mousavee Khan and Cazy Abdulazeez went together to the royal camp at Lodyneoh, but the Begum had so inflamed the Emperor against Shahjehan, that he not only refused Abdulazeez an audience, but ordered him into the custody of Mehabut Khan.[1]

By the time the Emperor had reached Delhi, his army was very numerous, having been joined by Rajah Nersingh Deo, Asof Khan and many other munsebdars with their troops. The command of the main body was given to Mehabut Khan; and Abdullah Khan was sent before with a large detachment to procure intelligence, and to secure the roads and ferries. The Emperor marched through the city of Delhi and encamped on the banks of the Jumna.[2]

When Shahjehan advanced to Belootchpoor, the two armies were within ten cose of each other.[3] Those who hoped to mend their desperate fortunes by a civil war, told Shahjehan, that after the indignity offered to him in the person of his ambassador, there remained no prospect of any success from lenient measures; and as his force was now very superior to the Emperor's, they

[1] R. B. II. 250.
[2] R. B. II. 251.
[3] R. B. II. 254; Iqbal, 200-2.

advised him to come to an engagement immediately, and not to allow the enemy time to acquire strength by farther reinforcements. He rejected this counsel, and declared that he had nothing farther in view, than to effect the restitution of his jageers, and punish the Emperor's evil counsellors. In order to avoid a battle, he marched about fourteen cose into the province of Mewat. He kept with himself five thousand cavalry, and divided the remainder of his army into three bodies under the command of Darab Khan, Rajah Bickermajeet and Rajah Bheem, who were directed to harass the imperial army, and cut off their supplies ; hoping, that when they were reduced to distress, the Begum and her party would be alarmed for their safety and agree to his terms. The Begum sent Asof Khan to oppose these operations with a body of twenty-five thousand cavalry, accompanied by Abdul Hassan, Abdullah Khan and Lushker Khan. The Begum had imprudently given the command of the van to Abdullah Khan, who being disgusted with her measures, only wanted an opportunity to betray his trust.[1] His design, however, was known only to Bickermajeet, who not having time to communicate with Darab Khan, the latter made a powerful resistance, to Abdullah Khan's attack, and in the action Bickermajeet was killed with a match-lock ball.[2] Abdullah Khan having now discovered his intentions to Darab Khan, joined him with part of his force. The death of Bickermajeet threw the

[1] R. B. II., 251.

[2] And his head was cut off and exhibited to the delighted Emperor.

Prince's army into confusion, but they were rallied by Rajah Bheem, and night parted the combatants, without either side having gained any considerable advantage.[1]

The desertion of Abdullah Khan created suspicions in the Emperor's mind against Asof Khan and Abdul Hassan, and these fears threw his army into great confusion.

Mehabut Khan also, alarmed at the success of Shahjehan, and fearful of more desertions, set on foot a negotiation through Gazy Abdulazeez, whom he sent to Shahjehan, to assure him, that if he would lead back his army without committing any farther hostilities, his jageers should be restored to him immediately on his return to the Dekhan.[2] Although Shahjehan did not place much reliance on the faith of Mehabut Khan, yet as he earnestly wished to have his father reconciled to him, he marched back his army without any farther stipulations.

The Emperor crossed the Jumna at Agra and set out for Ajmeer; whilst Shahjehan proceeded to Mendow.[3] Shahjehan, on his return, gave the Government of Gujerat to Abdullah Khan.

Etebar Khan, the eunuch, in reward for having preserved Agra, was promoted to a munseb of six thousand zat and five thousand cavalry with the title of Momtaz Khan.

Sultan Purveiz joined the Emperor at Hindore and was received with great affection.

---

[1] R. B. II. 255-6; Iqbal, 203-4.
[2] M. J.
[3] R. B. II., 262.

As soon as certain intelligence was received that Shahjehan was proceeding to Mendow through the pass of Ghattee Chanda, the perfidious Mehabut Khan, regardless of the late treaty, persuaded the Emperor to send Purveiz in pursuit of him from Ajmeer. And accordingly Purveiz, under the management of Mehabut Khan, marched from thence, with an army of forty thousand cavalry, a train of artillery, and twenty lakhs of rupees.

At the same time that Shahjehan entered Mendow, Purveiz and Mehabut Khan arrived at Ghattee Chanda. Having now missed their aim, they resolved to march back to Ajmeer, and return after the rains. But at this juncture, Rustam Khan, who from a private soldier had risen to high rank, through the favour of Shahjehan, having engaged in a correspondence with Mehabut Khan, advised him and Purveiz, to push on to Mendow, without loss of time, assuring them, that when the armies were in sight of each other, he would desert them with his troops. Encouraged by this promise, Mehabut Khan and Purveiz entered the pass of Ghattee Chanda. Shahjehan placing entire confidence on the attachment of Rustam Khan, sent him before with a large detachment to impede the motions of Mehabut Khan, whilst himself prepared to follow with the main body.

On the first and second days some slight skirmishes passed between Rustam Khan and Mehabut Khan, in one of which one Munsoor Khan,[1] a Portuguese, who had deserted from

[1] R. B. II., 271.

Purveiz to Shahjehan, was killed on the side of Rustam Khan, and amongst the troops of Mehabut Khan fell Ajeb Singh with about two hundred Rajputs. It had been settled, that on the third day Shahjehan should unite his forces with those of Rustam Khan, and bring the enemy to a general engagement. But early in the morning before the junction was effected, Rustam Khan with Mohammed Khan, Berkundaze Khan, and several other munsebdars deserted to Mehabut Khan, carrying with them the greatest part of the detachment[1]; of the remainder many dispersed different ways and a small party returned to Shahjehan.

About this time a messenger, with a treasonable letter from the Khankhanan to Mehabut Khan, was intercepted; and Shahjehan in order to keep the matter secret, instantly had the messenger put to death. Shahjehan now crossed the Nerbudda and retreated to Asseer,[2] leaving Byram Beg with a sufficient force to dispute with the enemy the passage of the river. Shahjehan sent for the Khankhanan and his son, and without any preface shewed them the intercepted letter; at the sight of which they were so confounded that they were not able to frame any kind of excuse, upon which they were given in custody to Syed Mozuffer Khan.[3]

Shahjehan left the heavy baggage at Asseer, under the charge of Rajah Gopal Doss, and then

---

1 B. R. II., 272-3.
2 R. B. II., 273-4.
3 R. B. II., 274.

proceeded to Burhanpoor with his sons.[1] Here he was joined by Abdullah Khan from Gujerat.

Gujerat was one of the jageers of Shahjehan, and we have already mentioned that when he marched back from Agra, he had given it in charge to Abdullah Khan, who dispatched Wasedar, an eunuch, with a party of new raised troops, to take possession of the city of Ahmedabad. The Emperor by the advice of Mehabut Khan now conferred the subahdary of Gujerat upon Dewar Bukhsh, son of Khusru, with Khan Azem for his Etaleek.[2] When Shahjehan arrived at Mendow, he sent orders to Kinker Doss, brother of the late Bickermajeet, and Sessy, the Dewan of the Gujerat, to repair to him, and bring with them the treasure, with the golden throne inlaid with precious stones which cost five lakhs of rupees, and a sword belt worth two lakhs of rupees, both of which had been prepared as presents for the Emperor. Sessy, in order to recommend himself to the Emperor, resolved to oppose the new governor, and the day before Kinker Doss left Ahmedabad, himself, under pretence of going to Shahjehan, marched to Mahmoodabad, from whence he wrote to Nahir Khan, Dilere Khan, and Baber Khan, Afghans, and other neighbouring jageerdars, imparting his designs, and requiring their assistance, to which they readily consented. Salah, foujdar of Sircar Putten, and Kinker Doss, suspected his treachery, but he had a large force at command, whilst they were

[1] R. B. II., 277-8.
[2] R. B. II., 260.

totally unprovided with the means of opposition. Salah withdrew secretly with near ten lakhs of rupees, and joined Shahjehan at Mendow: Kinker Doss also escaped with the sword belt; but the throne was so heavy that he could not carry it with him. Sessy wrote to his confederates, that now was the time for carrying the scheme into execution. Accordingly, the next morning at day-break, they entered the city by different gates. Wasedar took refuge in the house of Sheikh Hyder, who betraying him to the conspirators, he was seized and committed to prison. Mohammed Tuckee the Dewan, and Hasan Beg the Bukshee, were likewise discovered, and shared the same fate. The leaders of the conspiracy broke in pieces the inlaid throne, the gold of which they distributed amongst their troops, and divided the jewels amongst themselves. When Abdulla Khan got advice of these transactions, he hastened from Mendow to Gujerat, with only five or six hundred cavalry, and after 20 days arrived at Berodeh. Sessy Khan and his confederates marched out of Ahmedabad, and encamped at the tank of Kenkeriah, with about fifteen thousand men. Abdullah Khan receiving intelligence of the strength of the enemy, waited some days at Berodeh for a reinforcement of troops, and when they joined him, marched to Mahmoodabad. Sessy marched to the town of Betowah, and encamped near the tomb of Kotebul Alum. Abdullah went on to Berantcheh, and Sessy to the village of Beload, when the two armies were within three cose of each other. The next day they both drew up in order of battle; Abdullah Khan had taken post upon broken ground, intersected with hedges of zekoom, so that he was not able to dispose of his men to the best advantage. The centre of each began the attack; Himmut Singh commanding that division on the side of Abdullah Khan, and Nahir Khan that of Sessy. Himmut Singh was shot and the elephants in front of Abdullah's line, frightened at the rockets, broke in upon their own men, and threw the troops into such confusion, that they were totally routed. He fled to Beroatch, where he stayed only three days, and then went to Surat, and from thence with the remains of his army joined Shahjehan at Burhanpoor, at the same time that the latter had retreated from Mendow. The Emperor raised Seffy's munsab from one thousand cavalry to three thousand zat and two thousand five hundred cavalry, with the title of Seif Khan; and Nahir Khan was promoted to three thousand zat, and two thousand cavalry.[1]

When Mehabut Khan and Purveiz arrived at Nerbudda, opposite to the post of Byram Beg, a brisk cannonade commenced on both sides, but Byram Beg had secured all the boats, and defended the fort with such obstinacy, that the enemy despaired of effecting a passage.

There appearing no proofs of Darab Khan's participation in his father's treason, Shahjehan released him from custody, and shortly after, upon

[1] R. B. II., 262-7.

a further conviction of his fidelity, was induced to set at liberty the Khankhanan and his other son also. Mehabut Khan, seeing the Khankhanan restored to confidence and favour, wrote him a letter, intreating him to mediate a peace, which being also agreeable to the inclination of Shahjehan he made the Khankhanan swear upon the Koran, that he would not betray his interest, and then sent him to Mehabut Khan to negotiate the treaty. It was agreed that the Khankhanan should not cross the Nerbudda, and that his two sons should remain with Shahjehan as hostages for their father's fidelity. As soon as it was known that the Khankhanan was coming to negotiate a peace, Byram Beg became remiss in his duty, of which Mehabut Khan did not fail to avail himself, and in the dead of night, crossed the river with his whole army; when the Khankhanan regardless of his newly plighted faith, openly joined the enemy.[1] Byram Beg overwhelmed with shame at having suffered himself to be so duped, joined Shahjehan, who did not think it prudent to remain any longer at Burhanpoor; but resolved to march into Bengal as fast as possible. He was now deserted by many of his ungrateful dependents. Mehabut Khan and Sultan Purveiz went after him as far as Ghattee Bhenker, thirty cose from Berhanpoor, but a heavy fall of rain spoiling all their ammunition, they were obliged to give up the pursuit.[2]

---

[1] R. B. II., 279.
[2] R. B. II., 281.

A. H. 1033—A. D. 1624

Shahjehan marched to the borders of Telinganeh, the country of Koteb-ul-Mulk and proceeded by the way of Masulipatam.[1] When he approached Orissa,[2] the Subahdar, Ahmed Beg Khan, nephew of Ibrahim Khan, Subahdar of Bengal, fled to his uncle at Dacca. Shah Kuly Khan was left with a force to keep possession of Orissa, whilst Shahjehan marched to Burdwan. Salah, the nephew of Asof Khan, shut himself up in the fort; but upon the appearance of a siege surrendered. Byram Beg was left to command in Burdwan, and Shahjehan marched on to Raj Mahl.

Ibrahim Khan having collected together a large force, proceeded from Dacca to Akbernagar, with powerful train of artillery, and the royal nowareh, or fleet of fighting boats. This place was originally named Aj Mahl, and when Rajah Mansingh made it the seat of Government, it was for some time called Raj Mahl, and afterwards Akbernagar. When Rajah Mansingh built the old fort, the river ran close under it, but afterwards retired from its bed to the distance of near a cose. Ibrahim Khan afterwards erected a tomb for his son on the banks of the river, which he enclosed with strong fortifications of stone. He abandoned the old fort, and resolved to defend himself in the new one, which was inaccessible on the side of the river, and from its situation might easily be assisted with supplies by means of the nowareh.

[1] R. B. II., 290-1; 298.
[2] Iqbal, 217; English Factories in India, 1622-3, p. 315.

His garrison consisted of near four thousand men, amongst whom were several Portuguese gunners, the rest of his army encamped on the opposite side of the river. When Shahjehan arrived at Akbernagar, he wrote to Ibrahim Khan that if he would surrender, he should have a suitable jageer in any part of Bengal that he might prefer; and that if he wished to repair to the Emperor, he should have a safe convoy upon evacuating the fort. He returned for answer that his gratitude and duty obliged him to defend the fort to the utmost extremity, and that he was resolved to die in the service of the Emperor, to whose favour and indulgence he was indebted for everything that he possessed.[1]

We must now return to the transactions at Court. When the Emperor entered the City of Ajmeer, he received intelligence from Agra, of the death of his mother Miriam-ul-Zemany, whose loss he sincerely lamented. Sessy sent him forty-four persons, who had been active in the late commotions in Gujerat, two of whom were trampled to death by elephants and the rest committed to prison.

The Emperor being relieved from alarms for the present, by the successes of Purveiz and the retreat of Shahjehan, resolved to make an excursion to Cashmeer, that he might avoid the summer heat of Hindostan, which always occasioned a return of his asthmatic complaint. He accordingly left Ajmeer about the end of November.

By the advice of Mehabut Khan, Asof Khan

[1] R. B. II., 299, 408-410; Iqbal, E. D., Vol. VI.

was appointed Subahdar of Bengal, and had actually set out for his Government; but the Begum being unable to bear his absence, as she really loved him, he was ordered back again.

Upon the death of Momtaz Khan the eunuch, Mocurreb Khan proceeded to the Subahdary of Agra. Allavirdy Beg, who had deserted the service of Shahjehan, obtained the title of Motakid Khan, and Rustam Khan was appointed foujdar of Kenoje.

In the Dekhan, Mehabut carried all before him. Cazy Abdulazeez, Shahjehan's late ambassador, being now in the service of Mehabut Khan, was sent to Adil Khan, who with his confederates had submitted to the conquerors. Amber sent Aly Sheer to Mehabut Khan, with a letter couched in the most abject terms, desiring permission to pay his respects, and to place his son in the imperial service. Cazy Abdulazeez wrote to Mehabut Khan that Adil Khan, as a farther proof of attachment, had appointed Moulla Mohammed Lahooree to serve under him with five thousand cavalry. The country about Malwah was yet hardly passable for the artillery; however, in order to satisfy the impatience of the Emperor, who had written repeated orders to that effect, Mehabut Khan sent on Purveiz, whilst he remained himself a few days behind at Burhanpoor, for the arrival of Moulla Mohammed and his detachment. Lushker Khan, Jadoun Roy, Oudyjyram, and some other munsebdars, were cantoned at Zuffernagar, for the defence of

Ballaghaut; other garrisons were distributed throughout the Dekhan; and Rezawee Khan was stationed in Khandeis.[1]

When Ibrahim Khan shut himself up in the new fort of Raj Mahl, Shahjehan took possession of the old one. He then blockaded the new fort, and Romee Khan, the commandant of his artillery, was employed in carrying on a mine, whilst a brisk cannonade was maintained on both sides. By means of the nowareh, Ahmed Khan threw himself into the fort, and raised the spirits of the besieged. Shortly after, Shahjehan detached Derya Khan to attack the camp on the opposite side of the river. Ibrahim Khan alarmed thereat, embarked on the nowareh with Ahmed Beg to engage him on the river; but proving too late to prevent his gaining the opposite bank, Ibrahim Khan continued in the boats to hinder any reinforcement being sent to the enemy. A battle was fought on the eastern bank of the Ganges, between Derya Khan and the Bengal troops headed by Ahmed Beg, when the latter being routed retreated to Ibrahim Khan who sent to the fort for succour. Shahjehan, having no boats was unable to send any assistance to Derya Khan, till the Telyah Rajah supplied his want. Through his management, one thousand five hundred cavalry, under the command of Abdullah Khan, were transported over the river, a few miles above Raj Mahl, and joined Derya Khan. Ibrahim Khan now arrived in his camp, and came immediately to action. He formed his troops into

[1] R. B. II., 295-6.

three divisions commanded by Syed Nourullah, Ahmed Beg and himself. The conflict was, for some time, violent on both sides. At length Nourullah was overpowered and fled with his division. The enemy then fell upon Ahmed Beg, who made a gallant resistance and received several wounds. Ibrahim Khan supported him for some time ; but there remaining no hopes of turning the fate of the day, his officers entreated him to retire, representing the rashness of exposing himself to inevitable destruction, but the gallant veteran scorned to fly, and said he now desired nothing more than to die in the performance of his duty to his sovereign ; being surrounded and killed, Abdullah Khan cut off his head and sent it to Shahjehan. The besieged were now greatly disheartened, and Romee Khan having set fire to the mine, effected a breach in the wall of forty yards and the fort was stormed immediately. Many of the besieged, from the dread of the unrelenting fury of the assailants, plunged themselves headlong into the river, and the greatest part perished; numbers fell by the sword, and a few obtained quarter. Meeruck Jelayer, one of the principal men of Bengal was taken prisoner. The loss on the part of the besiegers was very inconsiderable. Ahmed Beg fled to Dacca, the capital of Bengal, where Ibrahim Khan had deposited his treasure, and left his family. When Shahjehan arrived at Dacca, Ahmed Beg and his party made their submissions and were favourably received by the conqueror. Here, were found twenty-five lakhs of rupees belonging to Ibrahim Khan, and five lakhs, the property of Meeruck Jelayer and others; five hundred elephants, four hundred horses, with cloths, and Aggur wood of immense value. The artillery and nowareh were all taken. Shahjehan bestowed the following largesses amongst his officers: to Abdullah Khan three lakhs of rupees, to Rajah Bheem two lakhs, to Darab Khan and Derya Khan one lakh each, to Vizier Khan and Shujahut Khan fifty thousand rupees each, and a lakh of rupees was set apart to be equally divided between Mohammed Tuckee and Byram Beg, who were absent.[1]

Darab Khan, the son of the Khankhanan had remained in custody to this time; but Shahjehan now placed such entire reliance upon him, that he appointed him Subahdar of Bengal. He pledged his faith in the most solemn form, and for the more perfect satisfaction of Shahjehan, gave him as hostages his wife and daughter, and a son of Shanowaz Khan his brother.

Rajah Bheem, son of the Ranna, who had always faithfully adhered to the fortune of Shahjehan, was sent to Patna, whither Shahjehan followed in a few days. In the subah of Bahar, where lay most of Purveiz's jageers, Mekhless Khan was Dewan, and Allyar Khan foujdar. They never thought of putting the fort of Patna into a state of defence; but upon the approach of Rajah Bheem, fled to Allahabad, so that the Rajah obtained possession of the subah of Bahar without

[1] Iqbal, 220-2; Iqbal E. D. VI, 409-410; Khaf I, 344-6.

striking a blow. A few days after Shahjehan arrived at Patna, where many of Purveiz's officers joined him, Syed Mobarick, killadar of Rhotass, delivered up that important fortress, the zemindars of Jowneah and other neighbournig places came also with their peishkush.[1] Byram Beg was recalled from Burdwan, and made subahdar of Bahar. Abdullah Khan and Rajah Bheem proceeded to Allahabad. Derya Khan, with another detachment, was sent towards Manickpoor, and Shahjehan followed shortly after. When Abdullah Khan arrived at Chowsa ferry, Jehangir Kuly Khan, Governor of Jownpoor, fled to Mirza Rustam at Allahabad. Abdullah Khan followed him and encamped at Jhewsee, directly opposite to Allahabad. Derya Khan encamped at Manickpoor, on the banks of the Ganges, whilst Rajah Bheem advanced within four cose of Allahabad. Shahjehan took possession of Jownpoor.[2] Abdullah Khan crossed the river to besiege the fort of Allahabad; and Mirza Rustam prepared for a vigorous defence.

We have already mentioned that Amber had made the most abject concessions to Mehabut Khan, in hopes of being entrusted with the supreme management in the Dekhan, when he might employ the imperial arms, to the extermination of Adil Khan, and the establishment of his own power. Adil Khan entertained the same views against Amber, and was more fortunate in his negotia-

[1] Iqbal. 221-2; Iqbal E. D. VI, 410-11; Khaf I, 346.
[2] Iqbal, 222-3; Iqbal E. D. VI, 411.

tions. Mehabut Khan having now openly united his interest to that of Adil Khan, Moulla Mohammed Lahooree was apprehensive of danger in passing through the territory of Amber, in order to join Mehabut Khan with the promised reinforcement of troops; wherefore a force sufficient for his protection was ordered to escort him from Ballaghaut to Burhanpoor. Amber, alarmed at this junction, fled with Nizam-ul-Mulk, from Kherkee to Kandahar, a frontier town of Golconda, leaving his family at Dowletabad. They gave out that they were only going to Koteb-ul-Mulk, to receive a sum of money due from him for his quota of the expenses of the war. Mehabut Khan directed that Moulla Mohammed, with Sirbullund Khan, should garrison Burhanpoor; and that Ameeneddeen, the son of the former, should accompany Purveiz with a thousand cavalry. When affairs were thus settled in the Dekhan, they began their march for Bengal. Being suspicious of the Khankhanan, his tent was always pitched near Purveiz's quarters, and a strict watch kept over all his actions. When Purveiz and Mehabut Khan approached Allahabad, Abdullah Khan, on account of the smallness of the force, being obliged to raise the siege, returned to his camp at Jhewsee, from whence, accompanied by Derya Khan and Rajah Bheem, he marched towards Jownpoor. Shahjehan crossed the river at Benares, and shortly after was joined by Abdullah Khan and the two other generals. To provide against accidents, Shahjehan sent his family to Rhotass. Rajah

Bheem urged Shahjehan to come to a general engagement immediately insisting that a resolute attack would ensure him a decisive victory; but Abdullah Khan opposed this rash counsel. He explained against the folly of imagining that ten thousand men, many of whom were raw and undisciplined, should be able to combat with success, against forty thousand of the best troops of the empire, headed by a general of consummate abilities, long experience and undaunted valour. He recommended to him to avoid the imperial army, and proceed with all possible expedition through Oudh to Delhi, and again when the enemy approached that city to retreat to the Dekhan, for that thus by keeping them in continuous motion, they would be so harassed, being encumbered with heavy baggage, that they would probably conclude a peace with him upon his own terms; or if they should persist in continuing the war, he would then be in a better condition to resist them. The ardour of Shahjehan inclined him to follow the advice of Rajah Bheem, so that the prudent counsel of Abdullah Khan made no impression upon his mind. Before the proper disposition could be made for an engagement, the army of Mehabut Khan came in sight. Roomee Khan, with the artillery, was advanced at some distance from the army, and being surrounded by the enemy, was obliged to surrender, without having done the smallest execution, although he had discharged above a thousand balls. The whole weight of the attack fell upon Derya Khan's division which was soon overpowered and totally routed. Rajah Bheem, in despair, flung himself into the midst of the enemy, and was cut to pieces. The day was now irrecoverably lost—yet Shahjehan undismayed wanted to make another assault: but Abdullah Khan boldly opposed this unavailing temerity, and seizing the bridle of his horse, obliged him to retreat with the scattered remains of his army.[1] All the baggage fell into the hands of the enemy, who satisfied with their success, did not attempt to pursue the victory any further. Shahjehan by forced marches reached Rhotass where he remained three days during which time Sultan Morad Bukhsh was born there. From hence Shahjehan sent an account of his defeat to Darab Khan, and directed him to hasten to Ghurree. But this ungrateful and perfidious man, forgetting the favours he had received from his prince, and regardless of his plighted faith, looked only to his immediate interest, and wrote word to Shahjehan, that the zemindars having risen, held him prisoner, so that it was impossible for him to repair to the appointed rendezvous. The affairs of Shahjehan being totally ruined by his late defeat, and the defection of Darab Khan, he stayed only three days at Rhotass, after which he set out for the Dekhan,[2] through Bengal and Cuttack, leaving behind Abdullah Khan with the new born prince. The nephew of Darab Khan, who had been given as an hostage for his fidelity,

[1] Shahjehan's horse was wounded. R.B. II., 294-6 ; Iqbal 229-34.
[2] Iqbal. 233-4 : 238-9 ; E. D. VI. 414, 416.

was now put to death, in revenge for his uncle's treachery.

TRANSACTIONS AT COURT. Whilst the Emperor was at Cashmeer, Khanehzad Khan, son of Mehabut Khan, gained a considerable victory over the Uzbecks in Cabul. Afzul Khan, whom Shahjehan had left at Bejapoor, now joined Jehangir, and was received into his service with distinguished marks of favour.[1] In the winter Jehangir returned to Lahore, where he received intelligence of the defeat of Shahjehan, on which occasion the munseb of Mehabut Khan was raised to seven thousand zat and seven thousand cavalry of two and three horses, with the Toman Towgh.

In the Dekhan, Amber received from Kotb-ul-Mulk the money due, and they renewed their confederacy with an oath. They then marched with a large force against Adil Khan, who being unprepared for such an attack, was obliged to shut himself up in Bejapoor, and then sent advice of his situation to Mehabut Khan, who wrote orders to all the munsebdars in the Dekhan to march to his relief. On their approach, Amber raised the siege, and retreated to his own country where he was pursued by Moulla Mohammed, but who acted with such want of caution, that Amber surprised his camp, put him to death, and took a great number of prisoners, of whom were twenty-five principal officers belonging to Adil Khan, and also Fereed Khan, whom he immediately ordered

[1] Iqbal, 248.

to be put to death. Of the imperial munsebdars taken prisoners were Lushker Khan, Mirza Manucheher, and Akeedut Khan. Amber sent the prisoners in chain to Dowletabad. Khenjir Khan fled to Ahmednagar, and put it in a posture of defence. Amber soon after appeared before the place, but his cannon being too small to have any effect upon the fortifications, he turned the siege into a blockade. He then besieged Adil Khan in Bejapoor, and possessed himself of the whole territory of Ballaghaut. He likewise invested the fort of Shoolapoor,[1] which had ever been a subject of contention between Adil Khan and Nizam-ul-Mulk, and the large gun called Mulkmydan-being brought from Dowletabad a breach was effected and the place taken by storm. He then sent Yacoob Khan, acossree, with a large force against Burhanpoor.

In Bengal, the zemindars delivered up Darab Khan to the Emperor, who was so enraged at the duplicity of his conduct, that he ordered Mehabut Khan to send him his head, and which command was accordingly obeyed. Khanezad Khan was now appointed Subahdar of Bengal. Abdulraheem the late Khankhanan was ordered to court. Mukhliss Khan was now sent from Lahore to hasten the march of Purveiz against Shahjehan.

When Shahjehan returned to the Dekhan Amber sent him the strongest assurances of obedience and support, and entreated him to hasten to Burhanpoor, which was still besieged by

[1] Iqbal, 236-7; E. D. VI. 415; Khaf I, 348.

Yacoob Khan, who had orders to surrender to him all the territory of Ballaghaut. Shahjehan encamped at Loll Baugh. Rowrutten and the imperial garrison in Burhanpoor continuing to defend the place with valour and skill, Shahjehan ordered two assaults to be made on different places, at the same time, one headed by Abdullah Khan, and the other by Shah Kuly Khan. Abdullah Khan met with such a gallant resistance that he could effect nothing; but Shah Kuly Khan got into the fort, seized the citadel, and shut the gates; however, for want of support, he was at length obliged to capitulate. Shahjehan ordered another storm, but it did not succeed; many gallant officers and soldiers perished in these attempts. The besieged then made a sally, but were driven back with considerable loss, and amongst their slain were several Rajput chiefs, dependents of Rowrutten.[1] Purveiz now appeared on the banks of the Nerbudda, when Shahjehan raised the siege and retreated to Ballaghaut. Abdullah Khan being seized with a religious frenzy, left the service of Shahjehan and settled at Indore, to follow his devotions.[2] At the same time Nussaree Khan, another of his officers, deserted to Nizam-ul-Mulk.

A. H. 1034—A. D. 1624.

Khan Azem died about this time at Ahmedabad. His father was a native of Ghuzneen, and his mother suckled the Emperor Akber. Jehangir

---

[1] Iqbal, 243-4; E. D. VI. 418; Khaf I, 349-50.
[2] Iqbal, 244, 249; E. D. VI, 418, 419; Hadi, E. D. VI, 395-6.

was very fond of him, and took every opportunity of advancing his fortune. He was a great historian, an elegant writer, and a good poet. His body was brought to Delhi, and interred in the cemetery of Sheikh Nizameddeen Aulia. Upon the death of Khan Azem, the Subahdary of Gujaret, was conferred upon Khanjehan Khan; and Dawer Bukhsh, the son of Sultan Khusru, was ordered to court.

The Emperor returned to Cashmeer in the middle of May. Sheriar was then appointed Subahdar of Tatah. The eminent services of Sirbullund Roy were rewarded with a munseb of five thousand zat and five thousand cavalry, and the title of Ramraj, the highest honorary distinction known in the Dekhan.

Soon after Shahjehan retreated from Ballaghaut to Burhanpoor, he was seized with a violent fit of sickness and feeling strong compunctions for having rebelled against his father, determined to sue to him for pardon. He accordingly sent a letter to the Emperor, imploring forgiveness for his undutiful behaviour. Jehangir wrote an answer with his own hand telling him that if he would send to court his sons, Dara Shekouh, and Aurungzebe, and surrender the fortress of Rhotass and Asseer, he would grant him a full pardon, with the whole of the Dekhan for his jageer. Shahjehan went out to meet the Emperor's messenger, received the letter with the greatest respect, placed it upon his forehead, and prostrated himself upon the ground. He readily acquiesced in all the articles stipulated by his father the forts were delivered up, and his sons sent the Emperor with a peishkush valued at ten lakhs of rupees.[1]

At the same time, the late Khankhanan arrived at court. When he came into the Emperor's presence, he prostrated himself upon the ground, and was so abashed, as to be unable to raise his head, till Jehangir mildly told him, that whatever had happened was not to be ascribed to his own will, but to the inscrutable decrees of Heaven. He then ordered the officers to admit him to his usual station within the railing.

A. H. 1034—A. D. 1625.

Some time before this the Emperor, at the instigation of the Begum and her brother Asof Khan, had dispatched Fidaiy Khan to Purveiz, directing him to send Mehabut Khan into Bengal, and to take into his service Khanjehan Khan from Gujerat. Fidaiy Khan now wrote to the Emperor, that he had signified his commands to Purveiz at Serengpoor; but that he would neither consent to part with Mehabut Khan, nor agree to receive Khanjehan Khan; that seeing no benefit to be expected from accompanying the prince on his march, he had remained at Serengpoor and written to Khanjehan to join him as soon as possible. The Emperor now wrote in a very angry tone to Purveiz,[2] insisting upon an implicit obedience to his former commands, respecting himself, and adding that if Mehabut Khan did not choose to go

[1] Iqbal, 238-45.
[2] Iqbal, 245 ; E. D. VI. 418.

to Bengal, he must repair to court unattended, whilst Purveiz remained with the army at Burhanpoor. The pretences for ordering Mehabut Khan to court were that he had not accounted for large sums forfeited to government, by the dismission of jageerdars, and that moreover he had not sent to the Emperor the elephants taken in Bengal and Bahar. Arebdust Ghier was sent to receive his accounts, if he chose that mode of settlement in preference to rendering them in person to the dewans. Purveiz consented to receive Khanjehan and Mehabut Khan dispatched Arebdust Ghier to the Emperor, with the elephants, promising to follow himself.

A. H. 1035—A. D. 1625

The Emperor arrived at Lahore on the 30th of Mohurrem, or 21st October 1625. Abdulraheem was restored to the title of Khankhanan, received a donation of a lakh of rupees, with a jageer in Kinoje. Afzul Khan was appointed dewan of the Dekhan. Mirza Dekhanee obtained the title of Shahnowaz Khan.

Khojeh Birkordar having married the daughter of Mehabut Khan unknown to his Majesty, upon the discovery thereof, was ordered to the presence, where he was beaten, and then committed to prison.

A. H. 1035—A. D. 1626

On the banks of the Chenab, the Emperor received from Zuffer Khan the head of the rebel Ahdad, which was ordered to be placed over the principal gate of Lahore. The 23rd of Jemady ul

Sany, or 11th March 1626, he encamped on the banks of the Behut. The Persian Ambassador here took his leave, and received for himself, a khelut, a khenjer inlaid with precious stones, and thirty thousand rupees. Along with an answer to the letter of Shah Abbass, was sent a goorj, or mace, inlaid with diamonds, and a belt, valued together at a lakh of rupees.

Asof Khan had flattered himself, that by ordering Mehabut Khan to court, his ruin would easily be compassed, but affairs took quite a different turn from what had been expected. He was attended by five thousand Rajput Cavalry, resolutely determined to defend him against the attacks of his enemies. Although Asof Khan had been apprized of the manner in which Mehabut Khan was coming, yet he had made no preparations to resist him, blindly confiding in his own strength. When Jehangir was informed of the approach of Mehabut Khan, he sent him word, that until he had settled his accounts with the dewans, and had satisfied all complaints, he must not make his appearance at court.[1] The elephants were sent to the royal feelkhaneh; and it was ordered that whatever Mehabut Khan had given as a marriage portion with his daughter, to Khojeh Birkordar, should be forfeited to the royal exchequer. Fidaiy Khan was sent to receive the money.[2] As soon as Mehabut Khan arrived on the banks of the Behut, Asof Khan regardless of

[1] Iqbal, 252-3; E. D. VI. 419-20; M J. P. 198.
[2] Iqbal, 253; E. D. VI. 420; Khaf. I, 360.

the Emperor's safety, crossed the river with all the troops, his own effects and family, the royal treasure and the kourkhaneh[1]; Motamid Khan and the Meer Toozeh being the only officers that remained that night with Jehangir. Mehabut Khan, convinced that this destruction was fully intended, formed one of the boldest designs ever carried into execution, which was to avail himself of the present fortunate conjuncture and seize the Emperor. Accordingly, the next morning, he detached two thousand of his Rajputs to burn the bridge, and oppose any attempt of opposition from that quarter; then at the head of the remainder of his troops, he repaired to the royal encampment. He advanced with only two hundred men, armed with swords and spears, and passed into the harem. Motamid Khan, hearing a noise, went out to enquire the occasion of it and upon discovering the intention of Mehabut Khan, entreated him to wait till he could inform the Emperor of his arrival; but he and his party alighted from their horses, pushed forward to the royal pavilion and broke down the doors of the ghosul khaneh.[2] The Emperor came out and got into his palkee which was standing ready at the door of the ghosul khaneh. Mehabut Khan then made the koornish and zemeen-bose, and coming close to the palkee, protested that he had been driven to this violent step in order to preserve his own life from the machinations of Asof Khan; that

1 Iqbal, E. D. VI., 420; Hadi. E. D. VI., 396-7.
2 Iqbal, E. D. VI., 421-2.

he now threw himself at his Majesty's feet, imploring his royal protection, only, entreating that if the Emperor thought him deserving of death he might be executed in his presence. By this time, the tent was surrounded by the whole body of Rajputs. Of his Majesty's servants, there were present only Meet Munsoor, Jewar Khan an eunuch, Firoze Khan and two or three others, with Arebdust Ghier, who had secretly entered into the interest of Mehabut Khan. The Emperor was so enraged at the insolence of Mehabut Khan, that he twice laid his hand upon his sword with intention of putting him to death, but was both times restrained by the admonition of Meer Munsoor, who told him, in Turkish, that he ought to conform to the present circumstances, and leave it to God to inflict a proper punishment.[1] The Rajputs now crowded into the tent, and would suffer none of Jehangir's servants to remain with him. Mehabut Khan then desired to go abroad, where he would attend him, that the people might not entertain any suspicions of violence, but suppose that he was acting by the Emperor's orders. He offered his horse which Jehangir disdained to mount, and desired to have one of his own, which was accordingly ordered. His Majesty asked leave to go into the harem to change his clothes, but was refused and only allowed to wait till his horse was brought from the stable. After proceeding on horseback for the distance of about two arrows shot, the Emperor was obliged to alight from his horse, and mount

[1] Iqbal, E. D. VI, 422.

Mehabut Khan's elephant, with a Rajput seated before and two others behind the howdah. Mocurreb Khan now joining them, was permitted also to mount the elephant, but not till after he had received a wound from one of the Rajputs. Kidmut Perest, Jehangir's cup-bearer, scrambled up too with a bottle and glass and was crowded into the howdah with the Emperor. A short time after, Gudjhust Khan, darogah of the feelkhaneh, brought to the Emperor a female elephant, himself being mounted on the neck of the animal, and his son placed behind the howdah. Mehabut Khan suspecting that he would attempt to carry off the Emperor, ordered him and his son to be immediately put to death. Jehangir now arrived at Mehabut Khan's tent, where he was guarded by the sons of the rebel. Mehabut Khan, upon reflection, found he had done wrong in having neglected to seize Nourjehan Begum and therefore obliged the Emperor to remount the elephant, and return to the royal encampment to rectify the mistake. But the Begum had eluded the pursuit by crossing the river and joining her brother Asof Khan. This disappointment greatly disconcerting Mehabut Khan, he next repaired to the tent of Sheriar, and finding that he had also escaped, cruelly put to death Chekjee the grandson of Shujahut Khan who was also with the Emperor.[1]

Nourjehan Begum immediately on her arrival at Asof Khan's camp summoned a council of the

[1] Iqbal, E. D. VI., 423; Khaf I., 356.

principal officers of the army, upbraided them with cowardice and disloyalty in deserting their prince in so shameful a manner, and told them they had no way of retriving their honour, but by crossing the river with her the next morning, firmly resolved to rescue him from the hands of the rebels. The Emperor hearing of this resolution was alarmed for his life, and in order to dissuade her and her brother from an enterprise which exposed him to such danger, whilst he remained in the hands of the enemy, sent to her Meer Munsoor with his signet. Asof Khan, however, suspected the whole to be the contrivance of Mehabut Khan who, he thought, had compelled the Emperor to send the ring, and he, therefore, persisted in the resolution of crossing the river in the morning.[1]

The ardour and loyalty of Fidaiy Khan would not suffer him to rest whilst the Emperor was a prisoner, and therefore during the night, he collected together a small body of horse and led them to his relief. Finding the bridge destroyed, they plunged into the river. The stream was so rapid that six men with their horses were drowned, and of the rest only Fidaiy Khan and six others were able to gain the opposite shore. They proceeded to the camp, but finding themselves discovered, were obliged to retreat, and after killing four or five of the enemy recrossed the river.[2]

---

[1] Iqbal, 259-61; E. D. VI., 423-4 ; Khaf I., 366; English Factories in India, 1624-9, pp. 151-2.

[2] Iqbal, 251.

The next morning Asof Khan and Nourjehan Begum attempted to ford the river at the head of their troops, but were repelled with the loss of many men; and Asof Khan fled to his jageer in Attock with his son Abutaleb and about three hundred cavalry. The infant daughter of Sheriar, who was seated in the howdah with the Begum her grandmother, was wounded in the arm with an arrow.[1] Whilst the main body was thus totally routed, Fidaiy Khan and his division had gained the opposite bank, and driving all before them, repaired to Sheriar's tent, which was guarded by a party of Rajputs. A violent conflict ensued, and some of Fidaiy Khan's arrows fell near the throne whereupon the Emperor was seated, with Mukhliss Khan standing by his side.[2] Of Fidaiy's party were slain Syed Mozuffer and Atullah his relations, and his own horse received four wounds. Finding it impossible to effect anything he retreated to Rhotass, where he arrived the next day.

The Begum now fell into the hands of Mehabut Khan, but was well received by him, and from this time he treated the Emperor with all the pageantry of royalty; whilst himself, in the capacity of prime minister, made every disposition according to his own pleasure. Khojeh Abdulhassan, Eradut Khan, and Motamed Khan having sworn friendship to Mehabut Khan, were allowed to join the Emperor. Bysanker,[3] the son of Mehabut Khan,

---

[1] Iqbal, 262-3; E. D. VI., 425-6.
[2] Iqbal, E. D. VI., 427.
[3] Bihroz is the correct name.

was sent to besiege Asof Khan in the fort of Attock who surrendered upon his life being assured him.[1] The Emperor crossed the river Attock, and Mehabut Khan went himself to the fort, where he made prisoners Asof Khan and his son Abutaleb with Kuleeb the son of Meermeeran. He put to death Abdulkalek, one of Asof Khan's intimate friends, and at the same time was executed Mohammed Tuckee, who had been taken prisoner at the siege of Burhanpoor. Moulla Mohammed Tatahvee, who had been Asof Khan's tutor, was put in chains, which not being properly secured, fell off after a little motion; this Mehabut Khan attributed to magic and had him executed for practising that art.

At Jilalabad, some people of the neighbouring country paid their respects to the Emperor. The author of Ma-fir Jehangiry says that the religion of these people has a great affinity with that followed in Tibet.[2] They worship the image of a man made of gold or stone. They marry only one wife, unless she proves barren, or is disagreeable to her husband. If they were to visit a next neighbour, they go over the roof of the house. Their city has only one gate. They refuse no kind of food excepting pork, fowl and fish; eating the latter, they say, occasions blindness. They do not roast, but stew their meat. When any one dies, they put on him clean clothes and bury him with a bottle of wine and a cup.

---

[1] Iqbal, 266-7; E. D. VI., 428.
[2] Also Iqbal, 267-8.

The following is their form of oath; they lay upon the fire the head of a deer or goat, and when it is sufficiently burnt, hang it to the bough of a tree, where it is left, and they believe that whosoever violates this oath will suffer some great misfortune. If a father takes a fancy to his son's wife, the latter resigns her without murmuring. His Majesty asked them, what things would please them best, of all the productions of Hindostan? They said a horse, a sword, some money, and a complete suit of scarlet, all of which were given them.

His Majesty now appointed Saduck Khan Subahdar of Lahore, and he was ordered to punish Jugget Singh, son of Rajah Bassoo, for having retired to his jageer in the northern mountains. Jehangir hunted all the way to Cabul. He entered the city on an elephant, and money was flung amongst the populace, as he passed through the bazars, to the garden of Shere Ara. A few days after he visited the tomb of Baber, and other neighbouring shrines.

The unrestrained licentiousness of Mehabut Khan's Rajputs occasioned commotions amongst the country people, and also in the camp. A party of these men went to one of the royal hunting seats where the soils were spread, and some of the Ahdyans who were on guard there refusing to let them enter, were seized by them and put to death. Some of their fellow Ahdyans, with the relations of the murdered men, complained of this outrage to the Emperor, who desired them to point out the offenders that they might be brought to trial. They departed greatly dissatisfied with this delay, and the next morning a large body of them attacked the Rajputs and killed between eight and nine hundred, amongst whom were some of Mehabut Khan's best friends. Intelligence was brought him of the disturbance, but not daring to appear during the tumult, he concealed himself in the royal pavilion, however, through the interposition of the Emperor the riot in the camp was quelled without any farther bloodshed. In the country near five hundred Rajputs were seized and carried beyond the mountains of Hindukush where they were sold for slaves. Buddy ul Zeman and Khojeh Cossim were accused before the Emperor of having excited the tumult and their defence not being satisfactory to Mehabut Khan, he confiscated all their effects and threw them into prison.

About this time died in the Dekhan Amber the famous Abyssinian general of Nizam ul Mulk. He was a gallant and experienced soldier and possessed proper abilities for managing the turbulent spirits with whom he had to deal.

As the Khankhanan was repairing to his jageer, at Kenoje, Mehabut Khan sent orders to Syed Behweh, subahdar of Delhi, to seize and send him to court. He also sent orders to Mozuffer Khan, subahdar of Agra, to keep a watch over Dara Shekouh and Aurangzeb who were advanced thus far on their way to the Emperor.

When Shahjehan received intelligence of the rebellion of Mehabut Khan, he marched immediately to the relief of his father, through the pass of Nassick Terumbuk, with only a thousand cavalry, hoping to augment his force on the road. When he arrived at Ajmeer, Rajah Kishen Singh, who commanded five hundred of his cavalry, died, and all his men dispersed, so that Shahjehan had now only half the number, with which he set out. Reduced to this extremity he resolved to proceed to Tatah, where he promised himself he should be able to raise a considerable force. He marched from Ajmeer to Nagore, from thence to the borders of Jowdypoor, and then to Jesselmeer, the same that Humayun pursued during the rebellion of Shere Shah the Afghan.[1]

In the middle of May, the Emperor set out from Cabul for Lahore, and on his march received intelligence that Purveiz was dangerously ill of an epilepsy, occasioned by excessive drinking. Dara Shekouh and Aurangzebe now joined their grandfather, and were received with great affection.

A woman, at Agra, who before had three girls at a birth, was now delivered of a son and three daughters.

Mehabut Khan thinking that his power was now fully established, became vain and insolent, treating the omrahs with such contempt as filled them with anger and disgust. The Emperor shewed such a pliancy to his will, that he persuaded

[1] Hadi E. D VI., 397.

himself he had really gained his confidence; and in order to increase this opinion, Jehangir pretended to communicate to Mehabut Khan every design that was formed against him, one time advising him to be upon his guard against the Begum, who was plotting his destruction; and again, that the daughter of the late Shahnowaz Khan, wife of Abutaleb, threatened to shoot him with a matchlock, whenever she could find an opportunity. By this course, Mehabut Khan was lulled into a fatal security, persuading himself that whilst the Emperor was so much his friend, he had need to be under no apprehension of any plot being suffered to take effect.[1]

The Begum was industrious in improving every opportunity against him. She fomented the dissatisfaction of the omrahs, animated them to revenge, and stimulated them to retrieve their credit by delivering the Emperor from his captivity. A storm was now ready to fall, unperceived by Mehabut Khan, and even if he had discovered the danger, he was unable to ward off the blow; for the Rajputs, his chief support, were so much decreased in number, as to be no longer formidable. Hoshyar Khan, one of the Begum's eunuchs, had raised two thousand cavalry in Cabul, and when they were within a day's march of Rhotass, the Emperor suddenly ordered all his troops under arms on pretence of a review. When they were drawn up, Jehangir sent to apprize Mehabut Khan that the Begum was going

[1] Iqbal, 267-71; 274-5; Khaf I., 374-6.

to exhibit her new raised cavalry, and for fear she might take that opportunity to quarrel, advised him not to suffer his Rajputs to appear, and also to keep himself secure at home. Mehabut Khan followed the advice of Jehangir and did not stir abroad that day. Early next morning when the new cavalry arrived, and with the other troops were drawn up before the royal pavilion, Jehangir sent orders to Mehabut Khan to remove to some distance. Although he was not now at a loss to comprehend the actual state of affairs, yet not having the power to resist, he thought it safest to obey, and marched off with such expedition, that notwithstanding he was shortly after pursued by the whole imperial army, he crossed the Behut, without molestation. The two armies encamped on the opposite sides, and it is remarkable that Jehangir both lost and regained his liberty on the banks of this river.[1] Afzul Khan was sent to Mehabut Khan with orders to go and attack Shahjehan at Tatah and to deliver up Asof Khan, and the other prisoners, with a threat that if he made any delay in the execution of this last requisition, a force should be sent sufficient to compel him. He immediately delivered up to Afzul Khan the two sons of Sultan Daniel, but at first refused to release Asof Khan. However, he at last set him at liberty upon swearing not to molest him and consenting that his son Abutaleb should remain as an hostage a few days longer. Mehabut Khan, after proceeding some marches towards

[1] Iqbal 275-6 ; E. D. VI., 430 ; Khaf. I., 377-8.

Tatah, set at liberty Abutaleb, together with Budy ul Zeman and Khojeh Cossim.

The following arrangements took place on the Emperor's arrival at Lahore. Asof Khan obtained the subahdary of Lahore, and the vekalut with Abdulhassan for his dewan. Afzul Khan was appointed khanzaman, in the room of Meer Jemlah, who obtained the office of bukhshee. Mokurrem Khan was removed from Coach Bahar to the subahdary of Bengal and Khanehzad Khan was ordered to court.[1] A few months after, Mokurrem Khan going in a boat to meet the Emperor's sirmaun, was lost in a squall of wind. Intelligence now arrived that Mehabut Khan having quitted the road to Tatah, had entered Hindostan, and that at Shahabad in Bahar, Sefder Khan had seized twenty lakhs[2] of rupees that were going from Bengal to Mehabut Khan. Sefder Khan was ordered to send the money to Agra, and go in pursuit of Mehabut Khan, and the Khankhanan who had now a jageer in the subah of Ajmeer was ordered to join him.

A. H. 1036—A. D. 1626.

On the 7th of Sefer, or 18th October, Sultan Purveiz died at Berhanpoor in the 38th year of his age.[3] His body was carried to Agra, and buried in a garden of his own. The Khankhanan was ordered to send his children and family to court.

[1] Iqbal, 265-9 ; E D. VI., 427-31 ; Khaf, I., 386.

[2] Iqbal, 277-9 ; E. D. VI., 431, 434 ; Herbert ed. 1638 p. (*d*) says the sum was 22 lakhs.

[3] Iqbal, 273 ; 279-80 ; E. D. VI., 429-32 ; Khaf, I., 382 ; M. J. p. 205. Tod ascribes the death of Parvez to Khurram I., 294 ; II., 33 ; English Factories in India 1624-9, p. 152 ; Rev. Terry hints to that effect.

Abutaleb, the son of Asof Khan, obtained the title of Shayistah Khan. Mirza Rustam Sessevy was appointed subahdar of Bahar.

We left Shahjehan on his way to Tatah where he arrived with only five hundred cavalry and so dispirited, that he entertained thoughts of going to Persia, having formerly held a correspondence with Shah Abbass. The fort of Tatah was defended by Shereef ul Mulk with three thousand cavalry and two thousand infantry; he made a sally and was driven back upon which Shahjehan attempted to storm the place, but proved unsuccessful. He now fell back, which event, with other circumstances, made him lay aside all thoughts of going to Persia. He had heard that Purveiz's life was despaired of; and Nourjehan Begum sent him intelligence of the retreat of Mehabut Khan, and advised him to repair to the Dekhan, to be ready to defend himself against any attacks. He now took to his palkee, being unable to ride of horseback.[1] When he arrived at Gujerat, he received intelligence of the death of Purveiz, which made him hasten to the Dekhan, by the same route that Sultan Mohamed Bhuzneavy marched to the conquest of Sumnaut. He crossed the Nerbudda, about twenty cose from Ahmedabad, at Champaneer ferry, and passing over the hills of Jeeraey, belonging to the Rajah of Baglana, proceeded to Nassick Terrumbuck, where he had left some of his people, and there not

[1] Iqbal, 276-4; 280-2; E. D. VI., 429, 432-3.

being any house at that place, he went on a little farther to Khyber.[1]

A. H. 1036—A. D. 1627.

Imam Kuly Khan, king of Turan, no sooner heard of Jehangir's unkindness towards Shahjehan, and of the rebellion of the latter, than he sent Abdulraheem a man universally renowned for his virtue and sanctity to act as a mediator between the father and son. The Emperor was highly gratified with this embassy, and sent some omrahs beyond the borders of Cabul to meet Abdulraheem; and when he approached that city, Zuffer Khan the subahdar went out and received him with the utmost respect. Before he reached Lahore, Mousavee Khan brought him a rich dress which the Emperor had worne himself, with a khenjir inlaid with precious stones. Near the city of Lahore, he was met by Abulhassan, the dewan, and Eradut Khan, the bukhshee, who carried him directly to Jehangir. He was excused the ceremonies of the koornish and tesleem, and seated near the throne; fifty thousand rupees were ordered for his expenses, and the Emperor sent him, from his own table, fourteen trays of victuals, with a complete service of gold plate, which he was desired to keep.

About this time died at Delhi Abdulraheem, the Khankhanan,[2] in the seventy-second year of his age. He was one of the greatest noblemen of the

[1] Iqbal, 280-2; E. D. VI., 432-3.

[2] A. N. III., 583; Iqbal, 287-8; Maasir I., 50-65; Blochman Grandees of the Mughal Empire in Akbar's reign, 334-9; Beal Oriental Biog. Dict., p. 11.

empire, and had performed many signal services under Akbar. He was a profound politician, a great general, an eminent scholar and a good poet. By order of the late Emperor, he translated Baber's Commentaries, from the Turkish into the Persian Language, and was also well versed in Arabick and Hindovee.

We have mentioned that Mehabut Khan having quitted the road to Tahtah, had entered Hindostan, and was pursued by a large army. Thus driven to despair, by the Emperor, he resolved to throw himself upon the mercy of Shahjehan. He accordingly sent a faithful servant to that prince, with a letter informing him, that upon being assured of a full pardon, he would enter into his service. Shahjehan readily embraced this offer, and sent him a most gracious letter, with the impression of his hand to increase his confidence; Mehabut Khan with two thousand cavalry[1] taking the route of Rajpipleh, and the territory of Bihrjee, joined Shahjehan at Kyber. He presented a nuzzir of one thousand mohurs, and a diamond worth seventy thousand rupees, with other valuable articles. He was honoured with an elephant, a horse, and a sword and khenjir inlaid with precious stones.

As soon as Jehangir heard that Mehabut Khan had joined Shahjehan, he appointed Khanjehan Khan Sepahsillar.[2] Khanjehan had frequently invited Abdullah Khan to a conference, and

---

[1] Iqbal, E. D. VI., p. 434-n.

[2] Iqbal, 277-9; E. D. VI., 431, 434; English Factories in India, 1624-9, pp. 153, 204.

when he was at Indore, leading a life of retirement and devotion, sent him the most solemn promises of safety; relying upon which Abdullah Khan went to Burhanpoor. For some time Khanjehan treated him with great respect, and pretended to consult him upon all occasions, but one day when he came attended only by a single servant, he was suddenly seized and thrown into prison. Khanjehan wrote an account thereof to the Emperor who ordered that Abdullah Khan should be sent to the fort of Asseer. But this perfidy met with a just punishment, for three days after he was killed by the same Abdullah Khan, who sent his head to the Emperor Shahjehan.

In the beginning of March Jehangir set out for Cashmeer. He was now unable to support the summer heat in Hindostan, so that this journey was more a matter of necessity than any of his former ones. He celebrated the festival of the new year on the banks of the Chenab, and the next day proceeded on his journey.[1] Upon receiving intelligence of the death of Mokurrem Khan, subahdar of Bengal, he appointed Fidaiy Khan to that government, who stipulated to remit annually to court five lakhs of rupees for the Emperor, and the like sum for Nourjehan Begum.

Whilst the Emperor was at Cashmeer, he had a violent attack of his disorder, which the physicians apprehended would have been fatal. He, however, recovered from immediate danger, but continued for some time to have such a

[1] Palki was the only conveyance his health would now permit him to use.

shortness of breathing, that he found it painful to be carried about even in a palkee ; his appetite was entirely gone, and he even refused opium, to which he had been accustomed above forty years. He had no inclination for anything but grape wine.

Sheriar was now seized with a disorder called the daus'saleb by which he lost all his hair, and was in such a condition, that the physicians advised him to go to Lahore to try the change of air. Dawer Bukhsh, or Bolaky, the son of Khusru, who, in order to secure the interests of Sheriar, had by the Begum's contrivance been put into his hands, was now entrusted to the charge of Eradut Khan.

In order to divert himself, the Emperor went to see the sport of fishing at Matcheebawun, Atchewel and Weernag. From thence he set out for Lahore, and visited his favourite shooting place at Byramgullah. At the bottom of a high mountain, a wall was built for resting a matchlock, and the country people driving the deer down the side of the mountain, afforded Jehangir excellent sport in shooting them. It now happened that a foot soldier was driving a deer before him, and his foot slipping, he fell down the mountain and was killed, which so affected Jahangir that he left off shooting and retired to his tent in great concern. The mother of the deceased came to the Emperor, and although he gave her money to support her, yet he could never after be easy in his own mind. It seemed to him as if the angel of death had visited him under the form of this unfortunate man: from that moment he sunk into despair, and

20

his disorder increased daily. He proceeded from Byramgullah to Tahneh and from thence to Rajore. He commenced this stage, according to his usual custom, about three o'clock in the afternoon. On the road he called for a glass of wine, but was not able to swallow it, and was with difficulty carried on to his tent. He breathed with the utmost difficulty during the night, and expired on Sunday morning, the 28th of Sefer, A. H. 1037, or 28th of October 1627, in the sixtieth year of his age, and twenty-second of his reign.[1]

Jehangir, on his accession to the throne, displayed considerable talents for governing,[2] but from the natural pliancy of his disposition,[3] with his unfortunate addiction to indolence and pleasure, he became involved in difficulties, from which he had not resolution to extricate himself.

A. H. 1037—A. D. 1627

Jehangir possessed considerable literary abilities. He added some chapters to the Emperor Baber's Commentaries,[4] in the Turkish Language. He also wrote his own Memoirs in the Persian Language, containing a minute account of the political and private conduct of his life, from the commencement of his reign to the end of the twelfth year: they are universally admired for the purity, elegance and simplicity of the style; and he appears in general, to have exposed his own

[1] Iqbal, 292-3; E. D. VI., 435; M. J., 217; Khaf I., 338; Abdul Hamid E. D. VII., 5.

[2] Roe, 147-8.

[3] For his qualities and disposition see Purchas III., p. 1[illegible]; Terry p. 440, 389; Letters received III., 856; Roe, 105, 224, 257, 273, 325, 328, 338, 447; E. D. VI., 448; Pelsart 6, 52-3.

[4] R. B. I., 109, 110, 110-*n*.

follies and weaknesses with great candour and fidelity: when he had completed the memoirs of twelve years, he distributed several copies[1] of them amongst his children and principal officers of his court. He continued these memoirs, with his own hand, till the commencement of the seventeenth year of his reign; when, finding himself, from his ill-health, unable to proceed, he from that period to the time of his death employed Motamid Khan as his amanuensis.[2] The whole of the continuation is exceedingly scarce; the compiler of this history not having been able to procure a sight of any other copy than the one which was lent him by his friend Colonel Polier.

In proof of the honesty with which he confesses his follies, we shall shew in what manner he speaks of his addiction to drunkenness:—He says[3] that at the age of fifteen, he went along with his father to Attock, against the tribe of Youse Zie, when one day, having separated from him on a hunting party, and being exceedingly thirsty and fatigued, Shah Kuly, the commandant of the artillery, told him that if he would drink a cup of wine, it would completely refresh him. He followed this man's advice, and drank a cup of sweet white wine, which he found so delicious, that from that time he became fond of liquor, and daily increased his dose, till at length he expressed juice of the grape had no effect upon him: constantly, for nine years, he drank, of double distilled

[1] R. B. II., 26.
[2] R. B. II., 246; E-D. VI., 280.
[3] R. B. I., 307-10; Roe, 99. 190, 222, 226.

spirits, fourteen cups in the day and six cups at night,[1] which he says, were altogether equal to six Hindostan seers, or English quarts. At this time he had hardly any appetite, his daily food being a chicken, with little bread and some radishes.[2] By a continuance in this course, his nerves became so affected, that he was obliged to get somebody to lift the cup to his mouth. He then discovered his case to Hakeem Hemam, one of his father's physicians and intimate companions, who freely told him, that if he persisted in this way six months longer, his disorder would be absolutely incurable. Having a great affection for the friend, and confiding in his medical skill, he gradually lessened the daily quantity, and reduced the strength of the liquor, by diluting it with two parts of wine, and with the help of a small dose of philonium, at the end of seven years, brought himself to be a satisfied with six cups daily. For fifteen years, he drank at this rate, taking the whole at night, excepting on Thursday, the day of his accession; and Friday, the most holy night in the week with the Mohammedans, when he totally abstained from strong drink[3]; on Thursday he also abstained from eating flesh as well as on Friday, on account of it's being his father's birth day.[4] After some time he left off the philonium, and in place of it took opium. At the age of forty-six his daily dose of opium was

[1] R. B. I., 8.

[2] Blockman (Calcutta Review, 1869) has turnips.

[3] R. B. I., 20.

[4] R. B. I., 184.

eight ruttees,[1] six of which he took about an hour after sunrise, and two at nine at night.

His mind was strongly tinctured with superstition, of which we shall produce some instances.[2] The first public proof which he gave of this weakness, is described himself. When he was at Ajmeer, in A. H. 1023 or A. D. 1614, he was afflicted with a fever and a violent headache, which at first he endeavoured to conceal from every one, transacted business in public as usual; but in a few days this disorder became so violent that he was obliged to confine himself and consult his physicians. By their advice he abstained from the use of wine for three days, which, only serving the more to exhaust his strength and spirits they permitted him to take to it again; and in a few days he was entirely out of danger. As soon as he had acquired sufficient strength to enable him to go abroad, he visited the shrine of Moyeneddeen Chiesty, and as he considered his recovery to have been obtained from Heaven, through his mediation, he resolved to have his ears bored and wear earrings, in token of his bondage to this pretended saint.[3] Accordingly when he was perfectly recovered, he had his ears bored, and ever after wore a magnificent pearl in each. His example was eagerly followed by people of all ranks; and pearls, to a considerable amount, were bestowed upon

---

1 A rutty is equal to eight grains.

2 As regards his religious beliefs see Monserrate, Maclagen J. A. S. B. 1896, I., 53,55,62 66-7, 69; R. B. I., 246, 268, 361; II., 94, 95, 100, 176, 186; Roe, 270, 276, 278-9; Manucci I., 158-9; Letters received, Vol. IV., p. 10.

3 The Mohammedans have adopted this ceremony from the Mosaic Dispensation. Exodus xxi. 1—6.

them from the royal jewel office for this purpose.[1] Another instance is mentioned in Motamid Khan's continuation of the memoirs. When Jehangir intended to change the standard weight from thirty to thirty-six dams, he hesitated about making even such a trivial deviation from the institutes of Akber; till a fakeer, named Jadroop,[2] assured him, that in the pretended divine book of the Hindus, the seer is fixed at thirty-six dams, upon which declaration, superstition prevailed over filial piety; for Jehangir believed himself to have been actuated by a divine impulse and ordered the new regulation to be carried into execution.[3] The following is another instance of his weakness: at the time that Shahjehan stood high in his affection, the prince was seized with a dangerous fit of sickness; when his father made a vow that if he recovered, he would never again kill any game with a gun; and accordingly he religiously observed his oath for five years; but upon the breaking out of Shahjehan's rebellion, Jehangir thinking to bring divine vengeance upon his son with withdrawing his own engagement with Heaven, resumed the recreation of shooting.[4]

The author of the Khelaffut-ul Tewarik[5] suggests, that the beauty of Nurjehan Begum was the true fatal cause of Shere Afkun's death, and suspects, that the charge of treason was invented in order to persuade the world of the necessity of

[1] R. B., I 266-8.
[2] Roe, 343; R. B. I., 359.
[3] R. B. II., 108.
[4] R. B. II., 236-7.
[5] Delhi Edition, 446-7.

depriving him of his life in preservation of the public peace, and this idea has been generally taken up by European authors,[1] who have written of that time : it is, however, but justice to declare, that this is not an opinion generally received throughout Hindostan, and that no other Persian historian, whom we have read, had laid this imputation upon Jehangir.[2] The murder of Abulfazel is an indelible stain on his character, notwithstanding the pains which he has taken, in his memoirs, in pleading the political expediency of so horrid a deed.[3] From the beginning to the end of his reign, Jehangir's disposition towards his subjects appears to have been invariably humane and considerate. The severities that were exercised on the accomplices of Khusru's rebellion, were such as are usually inflicted on familiar delinquents, in all Mohammedan countries ; and these spectacles are the less to be wondered at there, when executions, equally cruel and diabolical, are exhibited in many parts of Europe, where the gospel of mercy is professed and established by law.

So long as Jehangir followed the dictates of his own judgment, by preferring to all other considerations, the ease and prosperity of his subjects, and whilst he vigorously enforced the wise laws of his noble father, his reign was

[1] Roe is silent on the matter. Peter Mundy (Travels II., 205-6) ; Della Valle I., 53-4 ; Terry (Voyage to East India), p. 403 ; Manucci I., 161-2.

[2] R. B. I., 113-5 ; Iqbal, 23-4, 55 ; E. D. V., 404 ; Khaf. I., 265-7 ; M. J. p. 76 (*a*).

[3] R. B. I., 25 ; Hadi, 10 ; Khaf I., 223 ; Asad Beg E. D, VI., 156-60 ; Takmil E. D. VI., 107 : M. J. E. D. VI., 442-4.

glorious and happy; but when he embraced the soft allurements of pleasure, and abandoned himself to indolence and dissipation, he became the dupe of an ambitious woman,[1] who, with a view of maintaining her own unlimited sway over the empire after his death, practised upon him the basest artifices[2]; she precipitated him into violent acts of injustice against a son whom he tenderly loved; and the intestine wars which ensued shook the very throne, and made the empire a scene of blood and devastation for the space of seven years.

Jehangir had three sons and two daughters, by the following empresses :—

By the daughter of Rajah Bhogwandoss, Sultan Nissa Begum, born in A. D. 1586; and Sultan Khusru, father to Sultan Dawer Bukhsh, or Bolaki, born in 1587. He died in the Dekhan, in the year 1622.

By the daughter of Khojeh Hassan, Sultan Purveiz, born in the year 1589.

By the daughter of Rajah Keysoodoss Ratore, Bahar Banu Begum, born in 1590.

By the daughter of Rajah Oudysingh, Sultan Khorum (afterwards Shahjehan) born in 1592.

---

[1] Roe, 325.

[2] Iqbal E. D. VI., 405; Hadi E. D. VI., 398-[illegible]; M. J. 76-[illegible], Terry, 406; Roe, 88*n*, 89, 235, 256, 270, 337, 338; Peter Mundy II., 206; Della Valle I., 54; Bernier, 5; Pelsart, 50.

REGULATIONS

ESTABLISHED BY

JEHANGIR

TAKEN FROM HIS OWN MEMOIRS.

THE FIRST YEAR OF THE REIGN.

The first order which Jehangir issued on his accession to the throne, was for the construction of the golden chain of justice. It was made of pure gold, and measured thirty yards, consisting of sixty links, weighing four maunds of Hindostan.* One end of the chain was suspended from the royal bastion of the fortress of Agra, and the other fastened in the ground near the side of the river. The intention of this extraordinary invention was that if the officers of the courts of law were partial in their decisions, or dilatory in the administration of justice, the injured parties might come themselves to this chain, and making a noise, by shaking the links of it, give notice that they were waiting to represent their grievance to his Majesty.

An edict was issued containing twelve general regulations, in substance as follows:—

THE FIRST.—Positively abolishes the collection of duties, arising from Tumgha and Meer Bhery; together with the taxes of every description, which the jageerdars, throughout the empire, had been used to levy for their own private benefit.

THE SECOND.—To prevent robberies, and for the convenience of travellers, it is commanded, that mosques and serais be built, and wells dug in all deserted places; and every encouragement given for people to settle on and cultivate such lands. If these places are situated in any of the jageer lands, those improvements are to be made at the expense of such jageerdars; but where they are

* About four hundred pounds avoirdupois.

part of the khalseh lands, the charges shall be defrayed by the officers of government.

THE THIRD.—That no person shall open any package of merchandize, in the road, without the express permission of the proprietor.

THE FOURTH.—That throughout the empire, no officer of government shall claim the property of any deceased Mussalman or Hindu, his whole estate, real and personal, shall be possessed solely by his heirs. Provided he leaves no heirs, then officers appointed for this particular purpose shall take an inventory of the effects; and the produce thereof shall be applied to the building of serais, repairing bridges and digging tanks and wells.

THE FIFTH.—No person shall be allowed to make or sell wine, or any other inebriating liquor.

THE SIXTH.—No person on a journey shall be suffered to take up his abode in the house of any man, *without his free consent.*

THE SEVENTH.—No Magistrate shall, of his own authority, order any one to be deprived of his ears or nose for the commission of any crime whatsoever.

THE EIGHTH.—The officers of the khalseh and jageerdars are positively prohibited from the practice of forcibly taking the ryot's lands and cultivating them for their own benefit.

THE NINTH.—No aumil of the khalseh, or jageerdar, shall contract a marriage with any inhabitant of his district, without his Majesty's express permission.

THE TENTH.—Hospitals are ordered to be erected in all the great cities throughout the Empire and the charges for attendance and medicines to be defrayed by the khalseh.

THE ELEVENTH.—In imitation of the late Emperor, he forbids the killing of any animals on particular days, *viz.*, on every Thursday, the day of his accession, on every Sunday, because he was born on that day, as well as on account of its being under the immediate influence of the sun; besides as many days as he should be years old commencing with his birth-day.

THE TWELFTH.—Confirms all his father's servants in their respective munsebs and jageers.

He also commanded that all prisoners should now be set at liberty; and that in future no person should be confined in any part of the Empire, above a year, without his knowledge and approbation.

He moreover directed the bukhshies to make enquiry and inform him, whether any of his father's, or his own servants, wished to exchange their present jageers for lands situated in their native country, to be possessed by them in the form of Altumgha, without being subject to any alteration.

The Emperors, his predecessors, whenever they bestowed a jageer in MELKYET or PERPETUITY were used to affix to the patent a red seal from whence such a grant was called ALTUMGHA.* Jehangir directed, that instead of red ink, the impression of the seal should be taken upon gold leaf, whence it was afterwards called Altoon Tumgha.†

The collection of Zekat which brought in an annual revenue of several crores of dams, had before been remitted throughout the empire, in confirmation of a regulation made by the late Emperor. Jehangir now abolished the Syerjehat in Cabul, which produced annually one crore and twenty-three lakhs of dams. When the Zekat was collected, it fell very heavy in Cabul and Kandahar; and the abolition of that tax, with the additional remission of the Syerjehat, were great encouragements for the merchants of Iran and Turan to carry on a trade in those parts that was very advantageous to Hindostan.

The following was another of this Emperor's humane institutions:—In every great city throughout the Empire, as well as in

*A Turkish word signifying the red patent.

† Is also Turkish, and means the golden patent.

jageer as in the khalseh lands, refectories were ordered to be established, according to the size of the place, where victuals were daily prepared for the support of the poor inhabitants, and for the refreshment of travellers.

THE THIRD YEAR OF THE REIGN.

It had long been usual in Sylhet, and other dependencies of Bengal, for the ryots to castrate their children, and give them to the governors of those provinces in satisfaction of their rents, or else to sell them. This infamous practice had, at length, become so common, that many thousands were thus annually deprived of their virility. To eradicate this evil, the Emperor now issued an edict, prohibiting all persons from committing this act of barbarity, and forbidding any one to buy or sell a castrated child, Islam Khan, the subahdar of Bengal, was ordered to punish, in an exemplary manner all persons convicted of this crime. He was also directed to seize all the castrated children he could find, that thereby an end being put to this cruel traffic, the offence might cease of itself, as the dread of punishment, and deprivation of gain, could not fail operating upon the minds of those monsters of the human kind.

The sale of bang and all other intoxicating drugs was now prohibited; and it was made criminal for them to be brought to the public markets. Gaming houses were likewise forbidden.

THE SEVENTH YEAR OF THE REIGN.

It having been repeatedly represented to his Majesty, that the subahdars of the distant provinces assumed particular honours due only to royalty; an edict was issued containing the following prohibitions:—That the subahdars and governors do not require the Koomekee troops to furnish guards for their own persons. That they do not exhibit elephant fights. That they do not punish criminals, by depriving them of sight nor by mutilating their ears or noses. That they do not make any one a Mohammedan by compulsion. That they do not confer titles upon any of their dependants. That they do not suffer any of the munsebdars to pay them the compliment of the koornish or tesleem. That they do not cause the nakareh to be beaten, at the time they are going out of their houses. That when they give an elephant or a horse to anyone, whether he be a servant of the Emperor, or one of their own dependants, he shall not put the trappings or the kudjek upon his neck, nor make the tesleem. That they do not suffer any munsebdar to go abroad in their train on foot. That if they send them any present, they do not put their seal upon it.

THE THIRTEENTH YEAR OF THE REIGN.

One morning a man was convicted of a capital offence; but shortly after having passed sentence, the Emperor was induced to mitigate the punishment. Unfortunately the favourable mandate arrived too late; the officer who had charge of the prisoner, having had him executed immediately on the receipt of the death warrant. Jehangir was greatly displeased at the officer's precipitancy; and in order, effectually, to prevent such a proceeding in future, he enacted a law, commanding, that hereafter no criminal should be put to death before sunset, notwithstanding there should be the most positive orders to the contrary, even from the monarch himself.

COINS STRUCK IN THIS REIGN.

Gold Mohurs.

Noursbahy, that of one hundred tolahs.
Noursultany, that of fifty tolahs.
Nourdowlet, that of twenty tolahs.
Nourkurrem, that of ten tolahs.
Nourmehr, that of five tolahs.
Nourjehany, that of one tolah.
Nourany, that of half a tolah.
Rewajy, that of a quarter of a tolah.

Silver Coins.

Kokeb Taleh, weighing 100 tolahs.
Kokeb Ekbal, fifty tolahs.
Kokeb Morad, twenty tolahs.

Kokeb Bukht, ten tolahs.
Kokeb Saad, five tolahs.
Jehangiry, one tolah.
Sultany, half a tolah.
Eisary, a quarter.
Khyer Kebool, the tenth of a tolah.

The Mohurs of 100, 50, 20, 10 and 5 tolahs have the following inscriptions:

ON THE SIDE THIS DISTICH:

In characters of light, in gold, with the pen of divine decree.

Are written the king, the light of religion, the conqueror of the world.

BETWEEN THE VERSES:

There is no God but God, and Mohammed is the prophet of God.

On the reverse the following distich, which expresses the year of the Hegira:

With this coin, like the sun, the world is enlightened.

The sun of the empire is the date thereof.

ON THE OTHER COINS WAS THE FOLLOWING DISTICH.

The face of the coin is enlightened like the sun and moon.

By Shah Noureddeen Jehangir, son of Akber Padshah.

In A. H. 1027, or 13th year of his reign, Jehangir commanded, that in future gold mohurs should be impressed on one side with the sign of the zodiac, in which the sun happened to be when the money was coined; and on the reverse the following inscription:

The face of the coin is embellished by Jehangir Shah, son of Akber Shah.

With the year of the Hegira, and place where it was struck.*

* Continuation of Jehangir's Memoirs.

JEHANGIR'S PRINCIPAL ROUTES

Extracted from his Memoirs.

JEHANGIR'S ROUTE FROM LAHORE TO CABUL.

The 25th of March 1607, Jehangir left the city of Lahore, and crossing the river Rawee, arrived at the garden of Dilamez, situated on the western bank of that river; where he remained four days. On Monday, the 19th, he marched to the village of Hirbir, three cose from Lahore. The next day he halted at the village of Jehangirpoor, one of the imperial hunting seats. He commanded Secunder, the Jageerdar of Jehangirpoor, to erect a strong fort at that place.

On the 1st of April, he proceeded to the pergunnah of Chandalla; from whence in two marches, he arrived at Hafezabad. There he halted two days, at the house erected by Meer Kovameddeen, the croree of that place; and then proceeded by two marches, to the banks of the river Chenab. On the 8th he crossed a bridge and entered the borders of the pergunnah of Gujerat. When Akber was on his march to Cashmeer, he erected a fort on the west side of the river, which he peopled with Gudgirs, and from this circumstance it obtained the name of Gujerat; and was formed into a separate pergunnah. The Gudjirs were before that time an uncivilized race, who lived chiefly by plunder.

On the 9th he encamped at Khowasspoor, four cose from Gujerat, and which was founded by Khowass Khan, the slave of Sheer Shah the Afghan. Two marches intervened between this place and the river Behut on whose banks he halted. The source of the river Behut is a fountain in Cashmeer, named Virnag, probably from a large snake having formerly been seen there. Jehangir says, that during the life-time of his father, he went twice to this fountain, which is about twenty cose from the city of Cashmeer; that its form is octagonal; about twenty yards in circumference. The vestiges of places of worship, without number, are to be traced amongst the ruins and caves, which are interspersed throughout this neighbourhood. This stream is much increased by the time it reaches Pampoor, which is ten cose from the city of Cashmeer.

In this quarter is produced all the saffron of Cashmeer; the annual produce is about five hundred maunds of Hindostan. Some of the saffron beds extend a cose, and others are of smaller dimension. The flowers look very beautiful at some distance, and when they are plucked, emit a strong smell. Jehangir says, that when he went to this spot, all his attendants were seized with the head-ache; and that although he was himself heated with liquor, his head was also affected, that he enquired of the Cashmerians, who were employed in gathering the saffron, how they found themselves, and they answered that knew not such a disorder. The Behut being joined in its course on both sides by other streams, becomes a considerable river; but its breadth, in many places, is not more than an arrow shot. The water of this river being turbid and unwholesome, is never used by the Cashmerians, who drink the water of a reservoir near the city, called Dell. The river Behut on its way to Punjab, passes through Burhamola, Pukelee and Dumtore.

The 17th of April, he marched from the banks of the Behut. The 19th he arrived at the fort of Rhotass, which was built by Sheer Shah the Afghan. It stands upon broken ground, in such a manner, that it is not possible to conceive a stronger situation. As this spot borders upon the country of the Teekhers, a lawless and seditious tribe, Sheer Khan resolved to build this fort to over-awe and restrain them. He died soon after the work was begun, and the honor of completing it was reserved for his son Sileem Khan. Over one of the gates is engraved on account of the expense, which amounted to four lakhs and twenty-five thousand rupees.

The 20th he marched three cose and three quarters, to Pulla, which in the dialect of the Geekhers, signifies a *bank*. The 21st he proceeded to the village of Beekher, which, in this dialect, means *a forest*. The whole of the last road lies by the side of a delightful rivulet, whose banks are covered with the kuner flower, which resembles the peach blossom; and the tree is always in bloom.

The 22nd he marched from Beekher to Hatea. This place is called Hatea, from its founder Hatee, a Geekher. The country which lies between Markula and Hatea, is called Bootewar. From Rhotass to Hatea, the country is inhabited by the Bhojials, a tribe descended from the same stock with the Geekhers.

The 23rd he marched four cose and three quarters, to Pucka. This place is so called from its having a ferry of solid brick work; PUCKA in the language of Hindostan signifying SOLID WORK. This road was so excessively sandy and dusty, that there was great difficulty in bringing on the carriages.

The 24th he marched four cose and a half, to Gour, which in the Geekher's dialect signifies BROKEN.

The 25th he encamped a little beyond Rawilpindy. This place has its name from its founder Rawil, a Hindu, and the word PUNDY, in this country language, is A VILLAGE.

The 26th the encampment was pitched at Kherbooza. Here, in the former times, the Geekhers, had a tower, from whence they used to issue and plunder travellers. As the shape of the roof bore some resemblance to a musk melon, it was therefore called Kherbooza.

The 27th he proceeded to Calapanee, which, in the Hindu language means *black water*. Here stands the small fort of Markulla. This a compound of the words *mar* and *kulla*, signifying *beat the caravan*; this being the place where the caravans were generally attacked. It is the boundary of the country of the Geekhers. They are a strange people, perpetually involved in quarrels amongst themselves; and all the Emperor's efforts to reconcile them were fruitless.

The 28th he proceeded to Baba Hussain Abdal. At the distance of a cose to the eastward of this place, is a cascade, which precipitates itself with great violence. Throughout the whole road to Cabul, there is not such another cascade, but there are two or three like it, in the road to Cashmeer. Near the fountain, from whence this cascade has its source, Rajah Mansingh erected a small edifice. Jehangir says, he enquired of historians, as well as of the natives of this place, regarding Hussein Abdal, but could get no satisfactory information who he was. The place which bears his name, is a pure fountain gushing from the skirt of a little hill.

Here Khojeh Shemseddeen Khowaky, who for some time acted as Vizier to Akber, built a brick terrace, in the centre whereof is a reservoir, into which the stream flows, and from whence it is conveyed for watering the adjacent gardens and fields. By the side of the terrace he erected a tomb for his interment; but it was not his lot to be buried there. Hakeem Abulfutteh Ghilany, and his brother Hakeem Hemam, who were intimate friends of the Emperor Akber, were interred in that sepulchre.

On the 1st of May, he encamped at Amrohee, upon a beautiful verdant lawn, perfectly level. At this place, and its neighbourhood, were about seven or eight thousand houses, the residence of the Delzaks, a tribe of Afghans, who were guilty of every species of oppression and outrage. Jehangir now committed to the charge of Zuffer Khan, Sircar Attock; and ordered, that before the return of the royal standard from Cabul, the whole tribe of Delzaks, should be driven to Lahore, and that their Kheters, or chiefs should be seized and imprisoned.

The 3rd, he proceeded on his march, and the day after encamped near the fort of Attock, on the banks of the Neelab. This fort was erected by Akber, under the immediate direction of Khojeh Shemseddeen Khowaky. It is very strong. At this time the water of the Neelab was so low, that it required only eighteen boats to construct a bridge over it. As the province of Cabul was incapable of maintaining a large army, the Emperor gave orders to the bukhshees, that only his immediate attendants, and particular officers, should cross the river, and that the camp should remain at Attock till his return.

The 5th, Jehangir accompanied by the princes and some of his familiar companions, passed over the Neelab, in a Jaalah, and alighted on the banks of the river Kama, which runs by Jilalabad.

A jaalah is a float, constructed of bamboos and straw, buoyed up earthern pots. In this country it is called seal; and in rivers where there are rocks, it is much safer than a boat. From hence he proceeded, after two days journey, to the ferry of Barreh. Opposite to this place, on the other side of the river Kama, is a fort which was erected by Zein Khan Koka, when he was sent against the Afghans of Yousef Zie. He expended upon it fifty thousand rupees, and called it Noushehr, or the new city. Humayun used to hunt wolves at this place; and Akber told Jehangir that he had accompanied him two or three times to see this sport.

The 11th, he proceeded to Dowletabad, and the next day encamped near a garden planted by Sheer Khan, in the environs of Peishore. Gowr Keteree, a celebrated place of worship of the Joegees, is situated in this neighbourhood.

The 27th, he arrived at Soorkhab, and from thence proceeded to Chucdoolick. Here he saw a great deal of the wood called Baloot, which is excellent fuel. The whole of this stage is over a hard rock, but not uneven or broken.

The 28th, he came to Ab Bereck; the next day arrived at the new royal palace; and on the 30th at little Cabul, from whence he proceeded to Negramy.

The 3rd, of June after crossing the bridge of Mustan, he arrived at the garden of Shehr Ara, and all the way he went this day, money was flung to the populace. This garden pleased him very much, and as it was Thursday, the day of his accession, he invited his intimates to a banquet of wine. To add to their merriment, he challenged such of them as were nearly of his own age, to jump over a rivulet, about four yards wide. Some fell into the water; he leaped it, but remarks, that it was not with that ability with which he had exhibited there, in the presence of his father, about eight years before.

The garden was afterwards improved by the addition of some adjoining lands, which Jehangir purchased from the proprietors.

JEHANGIR'S ROUTE FROM AJMEER TO MANDOW

Extracted from his own Memoirs.

	Cose.
October 30th, he marched from Ajmeer to Rewary; halted there seven-days ...	1
Nov. 7th to Dessahwalee, halted here three days ...	2 3/8
11th to Madhel ...	2 1/4
12th to Ramsir ...	1 1/2

This being the Taluk of Nourjehan Begum, she gave a magnificent entertainment, and the army halted here eight days. During the halting days his Majesty made excursions upon the water; some boats being always brought along with the army, upon carriages.

	Cose.
Nov. 21st To Belood, halted two days ...	4
24th To Sahal ...	3 1/4
26th To Chowsah ...	2 1/4
28th To Deogong, halted two days ...	3
Dec. 1st To Bharmehl do. ...	3 3/4
4th To Kahil do. ...	2
7th To Lassah near the pergunnah of Bhoodh.	2 3/4
10th Hirdera, halted six days ...	3 1/2
12th To Sowreth ...	3 1/4
14th To Birdera, halted two days ...	4 1/2
17th To Kooshtal do. ...	4 1/8
18th To Khenlore do. ...	3 1/8
20th To Howeleh, halted one day ...	4
22nd To Ankenorch, halted two days ...	3 3/4
25th To Leyaneh do ...	4 1/2
17th To Gowraneh, on the river Chambal, halted 3 days ...	2 1/4
31st To Sultanpoor, halted one day	4 1/2
Jan. 2nd, 1617, to Manpoor ...	3 1/2
4th To Jarduhah ...	4 3/8
7th To Roamaneh, halted two days ...	4 1/2
9th To Kanhadoss do. ...	2 3/8
12th Through the pass of Chanda Ghatty to the village of Amjar, the boundary of Malwah.	4 3/8
Altogether Cose ...	84

The subah is in length, from Ghaddeh to Bensowleh two hundred and forty-five royal cose; and two hundred and thirty cose in breadth, from Chundery to Nuzzerbar. On the east it is bounded by Bandhown; on the north by the fort of Nour; on the south by Baghlaneh and on the west by Gujerat. It is a fine healthy country, well watered with rivers, and the soil fertile in most kinds of grain. There vines bear fruit twice a year, in March and and September.

In the town of Dhar is a very fine stone fort. The military force of the Kings of Malwah before the conquest by Akber consisted of twenty thousand cavalry. Mandow is the capital of this subah.

CONTINUATION OF JEHANGIR'S ROUTE TO MANDOW

THE MONTH OF JANUARY, 1617.

		Cose.
14th From Ajmeer to Kyerbad	...	3 5/8
15th To Sendhoreh	...	3
18th To Bejaree	...	4 2/8
20th To Bulbullee	...	4 3/8
22nd to Kuree	...	4 2/8
24th To Amerna	...	2 7/8
26th Marched. He has here omitted the name of the place as well as the distance.		
28th To Boolkehtery	...	3 5/8
30th To Cossimkereh	...	5

Here Jehangir killed a small white deer, with four horns, two measuring en two fingers breadth, placed just before the eyes, and two four fingers breadth farther back, measuring each four fingers breadth in length. The Hindus call this animal Dirdhayan, and say that the male has four horns, and the female none at all.

1617.		Cose.
February 1st to Cazeeyan	...	4 3/4
2nd to Kendawul	...	2 1/8
3rd to Culceyadeh	...	2

Here is a palace that was built by Nassireddeen, King of Malwah. It is surrounded with a moat. The Emperor remained here three days and gave orders for the palace to be repaired.

The 7th of February, he arrived at the city of Owjein. Here he saw the remains of an observatory that was built one thousand seven hundred and sixty-five years before that time, by the famous Rajah Bickermajeet.

On the 8th of February, the Emperor left Owjein and kept at some distance from the army to enjoy the sports of the field. On the 27th he encamped by a tank at the foot of the fort of Mandow. From Ajmeer to Mandow is one hundred and fifty-nine cose.

The fort of Mandow is situated on a mountain and is upwards of ten cose in circuit. The fort is very strong, and has in it a fine stone mosque that was built by Sultan Housheng. Here is the tomb of Nassireddeen who murdered his father Ghiasseddeen, in the eightieth year of his age. He made two fruitless attempts to poison his parent, and the third time he succeeded, by infusing some noxious drugs in sherbet. The old man suspected his design, but drank it off, praying God to forgive the parricide, being himself fully satisfied with the number of his days. This Nassireddeen peopled a city entirely with women, all the officers being of that sex. He is said to have had fifteen thousand women. When Sheer Khan arrived at this tomb, he ordered it to be beaten with a stick: Jehangir had the bones dug up, and ordered them to be burnt; but reflecting that fire is a ray of the divinity, he was apprehensive that this ceremony might be the means of mitigating the parricide's torments in hell, and therefore commanded that his remains should be scattered in the river Narbudda, to which element they properly belonged, for he was drowned. The story of his death is as follows:—

He was excessively fond of bathing and one day having dived in the moat of Culleeyadeh, and remained so long under water as to have become senseless, one of his servants, in order to save his life, dragged him out by the hair of his head. When he came to himself, instead of rewarding such a service, he was so enraged at the indignity of being dragged by the hair, that he ordered the man's hands to be cut off. In consequence of which, when a like accident befell him again, the attendants suffered him to remain under water till he was actually dead. This happened in A. H. 916 or A. D. 1510.

SUBAHDARS OF BENGAL

During the reign of

JEHANGIR

		When appointed	
		A. H.	A. D.
Rajah Mansingh	...	1014	1605
Kotebeddeen Khan Kokultash	...	1015	1606
Jehangir Kuly Khan	...	1016	1607
Islam Khan	...	1017	1608
Cossim Khan	...	1022	1613
Ibrahim Khan	...	1026	1617
Kanehzad Khan	...	1033	1624
Mokurrem Khan	...	1035	1626
Fidaiy Khan	...	1036	1627

SUBAHDARS OF BAHAR

During the reign of

JEHANGIR

		When appointed	
		A. H.	A. D.
Jehangir Kuly Khan	...	1015	1606
Islam Khan	...	1016	1607
Afzul Khan	...	1017	1608
Jaffer Khan	...	1021	1612
Ibrahim Khan	...	1024	1615
Jehangir Kuly Khan	...	1026	1617
Mocurreb Khan	...	1028	1619
Mirza Rustam Seffevy	...	1036	1626

THE

ARABIC, PERSIAN, AND HINDOUEE WORDS

WHICH OCCUR IN THIS VOLUME

A

Abdul Azeez.
Abdul Hassan.
Abdullah Khan.
Abdulkalek.
Abdulraheem.
Abdulrahman.
Abdulrezak.
Abdulselam.
Abdulsemed.
Abed Khan.
Abul Čossim.
Abulfazel.
Abul Hussein.
Abulmozuffer.
Abusyed Mirza.
Abutaleb.
Aby Aly Sina.
Adilabad.
Adil Khan.
Afghan.
Aftabgeer, a kind of umbrella.
Afzul Khan.
Aggur wood, Lignum aloes.
Ag Mahl.
Agra.
Ahdad.
Ahdyan, the plural of, vide Ayeen Akbery, vol. I, p. 250.
Ahmedabad.
Ahmed Beg.
Ahmednagar.
Ajib Singh.
Ajmeer.
Akber.
Akbernagur.
Akbernameh.
Akeedut Khan.
Allahabad.
Allah Beg.
Allavirdy Beg.
Allyar Khan.
Altoon Tumgha.
Altumgha.
Aly Akber.
Aly Kuly.
Aly Sheer.
Amanullah Khan.
Amber.
Amda.
Ameenedeen.
Ameer ul Omrah.
Amerna.
Amer Singh.
Annyroy Singhdelun.
Anowleh.
Anveri.
Aproop.
Aram Banu, "THE CALM PRINCESS."
Arebdust Ghieb.
Asof Khan.
Asseergurh.
Atagelu.
Ataleek.
Atcher Roop.
Atchewal.
Atta-ullah.
Attock.
Atyr.
Atyr Jehangiry—JEHANGIR'S OFFENCE.
Aumil, an officer of the collections.
Aurungzebe, THE ORNAMENT OF THE THRONE.

B

Baber.
Baglana.
Baba Hassan Abdal.
Bahar.
Bahar Banu Begum, The Blooming Princess.
Bahmenabad.
Bain Gunga.
Baisenker.
Balaghaut.
Balapoor.
Bang, an intoxicating liquor.
Barahmoolah.
Bareh, an Afghan tribe.
Bargee.
Bary.
Bedakshan.
Beejapoor.
Beglerbegy—Great Lord, Governor Turkish.
Begum—Empress, Princess.
Bhadre.
Behker.
Behow Singh.
Behut.
Behwen.
Bejaree.
Belood.
Belootchpoor.
Benares.
Bengal.
Berantcheh.
Berar.
Berkeh Serai.
Berkundaze, a man armed with a match lock, literally a thrower of lightening.
Beroatch.
Berodeh.
Betowah.
Bhelbass.
Bhirjee.
Bhogwandoss.
Bhojial.
Biah.
Bickermajeet.
Bokhara.
Bokharee.
Bolaky.
Boolkehtery.
Bootywar.
Budy ul Zeman.
Bukhshy—Paymaster.
Bukht ul Nissa, The Most Unfortunate of Women.
Bulbullee.
Bundeyleh.
Bungish.
Burdwan.
Burhamole.
Burhanpoor.
Byram Beg.
Byramgullah.

C

Cabul.
Calendar—A Mohommedan Monk.
Cambay, properly Khambayit.
Calmue, or Culmae.
Cashmeer.
Cazeeyan.
Cazy—A Mahommedan Judge.
Champaneer.
Chaul.
Chandalla.
Chegh.
Chekjee.
Chembel.
Chenab.
Chenghez Khan.
Chesmech Nour—The Fountain of Light.
Chittagong.
Chitore.
Chowdry, an inferior land-holder.
Chowgong.
Chowsa.
Cose, about 2½ English Statute miles.
Cossimkerch.
Crore—100 lakhs.
Croree—an officer of the collections.

Culeyadeh.
Culpee.
Currukpoor or Kherekpoor.
Cushtwar.
Cutteck.
Cutwal—Superintendent of the Police.

D

Dacca.
Dam—a copper coin, the 40th part of a rupee ; also a weight. Vide Ayeen Akbery, Vol. I, page 35.
Daniel.
Darab Khan.
Dara Shekouh—in pomp like Darius.
Darogha—Superintendent.
Da-us-Saleb.
Dawer Buksh—Goa's gift.
Dehwed.
Dekhan.
Delhy.
Dell.
Derya Khan.
Dewan—the officer who keeps the accounts of great men.
Dewan Azem, or Vizier.
Dey—a Persian month.
Dhar.
Dhoolpoor.
Dilamez.
Dilawer Khan.
Dilere Khan.
Dirdhayen.
Dirjen Sal.
Dirveish—a hermit.
Doast Mohammed.
Doonyadar—the title given to the Zemindar of the Dekhan in the reign of Jehangir.
Dowleb.
Dowletabad.
Duab—the country situated between two rivers.
Dull.
Dumtore.
Durgah.
Dyanet Khan.

E

Ehtemam Khan.
Emir.
Eradut Khan.
Etaleek—vide Ataleek.
Etawah.
Etebar Khan.
Etekad Khan.
Etemadeddowlah.
Etemad Khan.
Etemad Roy.

F

Fakeer—a mendicant.
Feelkaneh—vide Ayeen Akbery Vol. I, page 146.
Ferah
Fereedabad.
Fereed Khan.
Fidaiy Khan.
Firman, Grant, patent mandate.
Firoze Jung.
Firoze Khan.
Firzend—son.
Futteh Jung.
Futtehabad or the City of Victory.

G

Ganges.
Geekher.
Geeranbar.
Ghattee Bhenker.
Ghattee Chanda.
Ghiass Beg.
Ghiasseddeen.
Ghiass Zein Khan.
Ghosul Khaneh, the bath.
Ghurry.
Ghuzneen.
Girdabad.
Goa.
Golconda.

Gookerah.
Goorgan.
Goorjhek—nundineh.
Goorz—a mace.
Gopaul Doss.
Gour.
Govindwal.
Gowkundeh.
Grab—a Malabar Vessel.
Gualiar.
Gudjer.
Gudjhust Khan.
Gujerat.
Gujnal.
Gurjestan.

H

Hafezabad.
Hafez Jemal.
Hakeem Hemam.
Haram.
Haroon.
Hassam Bannarassy.
Hassan Beg Bedakhshee.
Hatea.
Hemayun.
Herat.
Hillal Khan.
Himmut Singh.
Hindookush.
Hindore.
Hindostan.
Hindovee.
Hirdoss Jahleh.
Hirhir.
Hissar.
Hoshyar Khan.
Houshing.
Howdah—o[illegible] more properly Howdej, is a seat placed on the back of an elephant.
Howrel.
Hussein Khan.
Hyder Beg.

I

Ibrahim Khan.
Imam Kuly Khan.
Indore.
Iraky—from either of the Iraks.
Iran—the Persian Empire at large.
Irej.
Islam Khan.
Iybek Khan.

J

Jadown You.
Jadroop.
Jaffer Beg Asof Khan.
Jageer—an assignment of land of military service.
Jami.
Jan Beg.
Jehan Ara—The Ornament of the World.
Jehandar.
Jehangir.
Jehangirabad.
Jehangir Kuly Khan.
Jehangirpoor.
Jemady ul Awwel—an Arabian month.
Jemady ul Sany—An Arabian month.
Jeraey.
Jerokha—vide Ayeen Akbery, Vol. I, p. 69.
Jerokha Dursan.
Jesselmeer.
Jewar Khan.
Jhewsee.
Jilal.
Jilalabad.
Jowaleh Mukkee.
Jowdhypoor.
Jowneah.
Jownpoor or Jewunpoor.
Juggernaut or Juggenaut.
Jugget Singh.
Jumnah or Jown.
Jungle—wild country.

K

Kaim Khan Arab.
Kamran.
Kandahar.

Kandahar—a frontier town of Golconda, some call it Kandhar.
Kangerah.
Kateb Mohammed.
Kelañore.
Keleetch Khan.
Kella—a fort.
Kelladar—governor of a fort.
Kemal.
Kendawul.
Kenkeriah.
Kenoje.
Kepuah—a long sword.
Keysoodoss.
Khaey.
Khan—lord.
Khan Alum.
Khan Azem.
Khandeis.
Khandowran.
Khañehzad Khan.
Khanjehan Khan.
Khankhanan.
Khansaman—steward of the household.
Kheleel Beg.
Kheleel Mirza Sharokhee.
Khellaffut ul Tewarik.
Khelseh—the exchequer.
Khelut.
Khenjer—a dagger.
Kherbooza.
Kherkee.
Kherwar.
Khenjer Khan.
Khidmut Perest.
Khojegee Futtehullah.
Khojeh Birghoordar.
Khojeh Cossim.
Khojeh Hassan.
Khojeh Moyeneddeen Cheishty.
Khojeh Wiess.
Khooshab.
Khooshkhubber Khan.
Khorasan.
Khotbah or prayer for the king.
Khowasspoor.
Khusro.
Khyber.
Khyzer Khan.
Kinker Doss.
Kishengung.
Kishensingh.
Koka—an abbreviation of Kokultash.
Kokultash—is a Turkish word signifying foster-brother.
Koomekee—vide Ayeen Akbery, Vol. I, p. 238.
Koornish—vide Ayeen Akbery, Vol. I, p. 207.
Koran.
Koteb.
Kotebaddeen.
Koteb ul Alum.
Koteb ul Mulk.
Kourkhaneh, the armoury.
Kudjek, an iron spike used for driving an elephant.
Kuneer.
Kurree.
Kuttore.

L

Lahoor.
Lallah Beg—called also Lallah Bazbehadre.
Lodehneh.
Loll Baugh.
Lushker Khan.

M

Madarun.
Masir Jehangiry—the History of Jehangir by Kamgar Husseiny.
Mahasingh.
Mansingh.
Manuchehr.
Mahmoodabad.
Maldah.
Mallick ul Vuzerah.
Malwah.
Mandow.
Manickpoor.
Masulipatam—properly Metchlyputten.

Matchubawun.
Maund of Hindostan is about 80 lbs.
Mawerelnehr, or Mehawer'l-nehr.
Mecca.
Meer Bhery—vide Ayeen Akbery, Vol. I, p. 290.
Meer Bukhshee.
Meer Jemlah.
Meer Jemaleddeen Hussain Anjeu.
Meer Kavaneddeen.
Meer Meeran.
Meer Munsoor.
Meer Saman.
Meer Syed Aly Hamdany.
Meer Toozek—vide Ayeen Akbery, Vol. I, p. 259.
Meeruck Jelayar.
Mehabut Khan.
Mehram Khan.
Mehr ul Nissa—THE LOVELIEST OF WOMEN.
Mehtra or Met-hra.
Mekher.
Mekhless Khan.
Mekran.
Melkyet, proprietary.
Mend.
Mendow—vide Mandow.
Mewat.
Miriam Mekany.
Miriam ul Zemany.
Mirza, is an abbreviation of Emirzadeh or son of an Emir, it is however a title given very commonly to Moghuls of inferior rank.
Mirza Birkhoordar.
Mirza Dekhanee.
Mirza Ghazi.
Mirza Hakeem.
Mirza Khan.
Mirza Khankhanan.
Mirza Rajah.
Mirza Rustam.
Miskal.
Mocurreb Khan.
Mohammed Ghuznevy.
Mohammed Reza Beg.
Mohammed Tuckee.
Mokeem.
Mollana Meer Kellan Hiravee.
Momtaz Khan.
Mongheer.
Monsoon—a corruption of the Arabick word MAWSIM signifying SEASON.
Morad.
Morad Bukhsh—THE GIVER OF DESIRES OR WISHES.
Morteza Khan.
Motakid Khan.
Motamid Khan.
Moulla Meer Aly.
Moulla Mohammed Lahooree.
Moussavee Khan.
Mozuffer Hussein Mirza Seffevee.
Mozuffer Khan.
Mugh.
Mulkmydan.
Multan.
Munseb.
Munsebdar.
Munsoor Khan.
Mustefa Beg.
Mustefa Khan.
Mymoory.

N

Nagh.
Nagore.
Nahir Khan.
Nainsook.
Nassik Turbeneek, or Nassik Terembek.
Nassireddeen.
Nassirullah Arab.
Neiy, a singer.
Nekareh, a small drum, allowed only to people of high rank.
Nerbudda.
Nereyleh Serai.
Nersingh Deo.
Nishapoor.
Nizam ul Mulk.

Noureddeen.
Nourjehan, or THE LIGHT OF THE WORLD.
Nour Mahl, or THE LIGHT OF THE SERAGLIO.
Nourallah.
Nowareh.
Nuskh—vide Ayeen Akbery, Vol. I, p. 128.
Nussaree Khan.
Nustalikh—vide Ayeen Akbery, Vol. I, p. 129.
Nuzzer, present, offering.

O

Omrah, the plural of Emir prince noble.
Orissa.
Osium, properly osiun.
Osman.
Oudyjyram.
Oudypoor.
Oudysingh.
Ouzek—vide Ayeen Akbery, Vol. I, p. 67.
Owdh.
Owjein, or Oujein.

P

Padshah Mahl.
Palkee.
Paniput.
Patna.
Peishkush—vide Ayeen Akbery, Vol. I, p. 27.
Penjab.
Pergunnah.
Phorloon.
Poontch.
Pucka.
Pucklee.
Pulla.
Pulwel.
Punpoor.
Punpun.
Purveiz.
Putten.

R

Rajah, an Hindoo prince, or sovereign.
Rajah Bassoo
Rajah Bheem.
Rajah Bickermajeet
Raj Mahl.
Rajore.
Raj Pipla
Rajpoot—vide Ayeen Akbery, Vol. I, p. 57.
Ramchund.
Ramraj.
Ramzan, an Arabian month.
Ranna—vide Ayeen Akbery, Vol. 2, p. 98.
Ranna Sanka.
Rawee
Rawel Pundy.
Rezawee Khan.
Rhotass.
Rhuntore.
Rokiah Sultana Begum, or THE ENCHANTING PRINCESS.
Roomee Khan.
Roshenrai Begum, or THE PRINCESS OF ENLIGHTENED MIND.
Row Maldeo.
Rowrutten.
Roysingh.
Rungteh.
Russoom Foujdary.
Rustam Khan.
Rustam Zemanee.
Rutty—vide Ayeen Akbery, Vol. I, p. 93.
Ryott, subject, peasant.
Ruby-ul-Awwel, an Arabian month.
Ruby-ul-Sany, an Arabian month.

S

Saiyeed Khan.
Salah.
Samarcand.
Sanjary.
Secunder.

Secundra.
Seena.
Sefdar Khan.
Seffy.
Sehareh.
Seistan.
Selima, or peaceful, secure.
Sendhoreh.
Sepahsillar—vide Ayeen Akbery, Vol. I, p. 366.
Serahperdah.
Serai, an inn for the accommodation of travellers.
Serengpoor.
Seyurghal—vide Ayeen Akbery, Vol. I, p. 288.
Shaban, an Arabian month.
Shah.
Shahabad.
Shah Abbass.
Shah Alum.
Shahbaz Bahadre.
Shah Beg.
Shah Ismail.
Shahjehan, KING OF THE WORLD.
Shah Kuly Khan.
Shahpoor.
Shahnowaz Khan.
Shah Shujah.
Shah Wallayet (Aly)
Shahzadeh.
Shahzadeh Khanam.
Sharokh.
Shayisteh Khan.
Sheer Shah.
Shehr Ara, or THE ORNAMENT OF THE CITY.
Sheikh, DOCTOR, LEARNED IN THE LAW.
Sheikh Hyder.
Sheikh Ibrahim Kurdoozy.
Sheikh Mowdood Cheishtee.
Sheikh Nizameddeen Aulia.
Sheikh Osman Haroony.
Sheikh Sileem.
Sheker-ul-Nessa, or THE SWEETEST OF WOMEN.
Shereef.
Shereef of Mecca.
Shereef ul Mulk.
Sheriar.
Shoolapoor.
Shujahut Khan.
Shukerullah.
Shumsee Towshekehee.
Sief Khan.
Sikry, a village where Jehangir was born.
Sileemgurh.
Sileem Khan.
Singhasen.
Sircar, a division consisting of a number of pergunnahs.
Sirdar Khan.
Sironje.
Sirrynagur.
Soliman Giranee.
Sonnassy.
Soobah, viceroyalty.
Soobahdar, viceroy.
Soob Kurren.
Soodra.
Soonderdoss.
Soorej Mull.
Soorej Singh.
Soorkhab.
Sultana, or PRINCESS, QUEEN.
Sultan Ahmed.
Sultana-ul-Nissa Begum, or THE QUEEN OF WOMEN.
Sultan Daniel.
Sultan Khorum,
Sultan Khusre.
Sultan Morad.
Sultanpoor.
Sultan Purveiz.
Sultan Sileem, or THE PEACEFUL PRINCE.
Summergurh.
Sumnaut.
Sundoly.
Sungram.
Surat.
Surbullund Khan.

Syar.
Syed, or a descendant of Ali and Fatimah.
Syed Behweh.
Syed Mobarek.
Syerjehat—vide Ayeen Akbery, Vol. I, p. 351

T

Tahneh.
Tank, a pond.
Tanka, weight—vide Ayeen Akbery, Vol. 3, p. 93.
Tatah.
Tatahvee.
Tehmuras.
Telinganeh.
Telya.
Tenab—vide Ayeen Akbery, Vol. I, p. 354.
Teriac, antidote.
Tesedduck.
Tesleem—vide Ayeen Akbery, Vol. I, p. 207.
Tibbet.
Timour.
Tirhoot.
Tooman Towgh—vide Ayeen Akbery, Vol. I, p. 65.
Toozek Jehangiry, that Emperor's Memoirs written by himself.
Towk Tomish Khan.
Tumgha.
Tunkha.
Tunnem Bahadre.
Turan.

V

Vakeel ul Sultanet.
Vakiah Navees.
Vekalut.
Virnag.
Vizier Khan.
Vizier ul Memalek.
Vizier ul Mulk.

U

Ulugh Beg.
Uzbeck.

W

Wefadar.

Y

Yacoob Khan.
Yeadgar Aly Sultan.
Yousef Zelekha.
Yousef Zie.

Z

Zat—vide Ayeen Akbery, Vol. I.
Zein ul Abedeen.
Zekat—vide Ayeen Akbery, Vol. I.
Zekoom.
Zemeenbose.
Zemindar, landholder.
Zemindary.
Zilhejeh, an Arabian month.
Zilkadeh, an Arabian month.
Zufferabad.
Zuffer Khan.
Zuffernagur.

END OF VOLUME THE FIRST.